The Road to wexcellence:
Leadership with Integrity

MICHAEL E. DUBYAK

ISBN Paperback: 978-0-9989966-3-9

Cover/Interior Design: Michelle Manley

Contents

Acknowledgements

I would like to thank the following people who helped me in writing this book: my wife, Denise, my daughter, Iva, my sister, Rita Malie, Rich Mintzer, Michael Levin, Parker Poole III, Hilary Rapkin, Row Moriarty, and Bill Ryan Sr. I also want to thank all former and current WEXers for their compassion, drive, and commitment in helping WEX become successful, dynamic, and independent.

I want to acknowledge my sister, Rita, author of two books, who passed away before my book was published, for her encouragement and support of the writing of this book.

I want to especially recognize my wife Denise, who has inspired me in so many positive ways. She has shown such compassion towards me and everyone she encounters. Her example inspires me to show more compassion to others in my life and to all human beings. She is young at heart and has worked purposefully to help me find my inner child that was suppressed for so long. Her positive emotional energy is liberating and encouraging to everyone who is in her presence. I am uplifted by her. Her insight has helped me navigate interpersonal interactions with more positive and mutually beneficial outcomes. She is my dearest friend, my loving wife, my travel buddy, my playmate, and my soulmate. I have a lot to be grateful for, most of all the love I am honored to receive from this beautiful dance partner in life.

Preface

A man's character determines his fate. The same can be said for a business.

It was the morning of February 16, 2005, and I woke in the Ritz-Carlton in the financial district of New York City. I was tired as we came off an IPO road show, which involved seventy-four meetings in sixteen cities in fourteen states over the past two weeks. It was a dizzying whirlwind of pitching our stock and our company's vision. That morning, as I opened my eyes, the world was a blur of both exhilaration and exhaustion.

It wasn't uncommon to forget what was said at the last meeting, or the one before that or the one two days earlier. Even though we knew our presentation by heart, repeating the same thing seventy-four times, the words and the meanings behind them started to blend together. We would finish a presentation and then in the blink of an eye, it was off to the next city where the whole process started again.

On top of the pure fatigue, there was an ongoing threat hanging over our heads, an unspoken fear that this whole IPO process could implode at any time. We could be pulled off the road show without warning by our parent company and told, "We're sorry, you are not going public. We decided to sell you to another company, instead." This would mean the IPO we were working so hard to achieve would not be fulfilled. It was a draining freeze-frame in time, both physically and emotionally. The road show had all sorts of other strange twists—things were happening behind the scenes that we were not party to or could not control.

Now it was finally the morning of February 16, and I fell easily into my daily routine: meditated, made my coffee, checked emails, read the morning papers, and finished a workout. Yet it was not at all a routine morning. I was in preparation mode, getting ready to have breakfast at the New York Stock Exchange, where I would be hosting some of the Cendant executives and investment bankers. Up to that point, Cendant had been our parent, but that morning we would be saying goodbye to them and the investment bankers who marketed this new entry, Wright Express, into the public market. Also at breakfast, I would be officially welcoming our new Wright Express Board of Directors and enjoying the big event with my executive team.

Today was *the day*. On behalf of everyone at Wright Express (or all the WEXers, as we called ourselves), including the management team and the new board of directors, I would have the distinct honor of ringing the opening bell at the

New York Stock Exchange. Following many years of working tirelessly to nurture the success of WEX navigating through all the ownership changes and experiencing the disappointments of the missed opportunities for independence, this day would mean so much to all WEXers and especially to me. February 16 would commemorate the first day of trading for the new NYSE-listed entity, Wright Express, sticker symbol WXS (today WEX). After so many ups and downs through the years at WEX, it was hard to believe this day had finally arrived.

After tying my tie, I pulled open the curtains in my hotel room, and there, straight out in front of me, was the Statue of Liberty. Seeing this symbol of freedom struck a nerve and unleashed all the pent-up emotion that had been building in me over the previous nineteen years. I completely lost it emotionally. All the fears and disappointments of the past washed out of me. It became so real at that moment: Wright Express, once a small, Maine-based business, had come of age and was finally going to experience a level of independence it had never had the opportunity to enjoy. We had tried over the years to secure control of the company, but disappointingly, we had failed. In just a couple of hours—when the clock would strike 9:30 a.m.—I was going to ring that pivotal opening bell at the NYSE.

My emotions were flowing as if a dam had breached; I was unable to control the intensity. I sat there on the couch in my hotel room and cried. For years, I had lived and breathed this story. The story had been my career passion. And today was the day for Wright Express to finally realize its independence after having six different owners. It had been a long time coming, and the journey had thrust my colleagues and me into a story with a dynamic and dramatic plot.

Ours was a story filled with many trials, tribulations, twists, and turns that I witnessed first-hand over my long tenure with the company. And now, the dream we had all worked so hard to attain was unfolding before my very eyes.

Like a person, a business is shaped by various factors: its parental influence, good, bad, or indifferent that is instrumental in shaping the business through its growth stages; its physicality, including products and intellectual capital that define it in its marketplace; and its culture, which is the personality that defines it, either sustaining its longevity or possibly limiting it. Unfortunately, for many startups, these influences and developments may end in the company's demise if any one of these factors is dysfunctional.

Fundamentally, there is no definitive blueprint for success. Every case is defined by the vision, passion, boldness, grit, persistence, luck, and foresight of leaders who are impacted by the parental influence, the development of the physical assets of the business, and the cultural personality that evolves and defines the business. All three of these forces provide challenges and opportunities for the leaders who ultimately define the persona and physicality of the business. We are who we are because of our parents, our unique gifts and talents, and the development of our own personalities, which is true of both individuals and businesses.

Leadership is a crucial piece of the puzzle. If one of a company's leaders is sufficiently determined and truly committed to its mission and the success of the company, and he or she is able to grow and develop as a leader, it will substantially help the business stay the course as it matures. Ideally such a leader could substantially help navigate the enterprise through its infancy, childhood, and adult stages. Of course, this is easier said than done. Finding someone who will persevere and who can manage and adapt to the maturation process of a business, with its ever-changing management demands, is rare. In this way, leadership is a lot like parenting: the ideal leader will be able to support and guide a business from its toddler years to the day it claims its independence as a freestanding adult.

This book describes how one small business located in Portland, Maine, survived and thrived in the wake of turbulence created by instability in those three critical areas of influence—and how it took a bold, calculated risk to rise to the top, persevering against the odds. This is also the story of the positive impact one committed leader can have on a company's journey.

My goal in writing the book is to capture, and share, this remarkable story of a company that experienced all the stages of nurturing and maturing that a successful business has to pass through, plus its own unique challenges and successes. I have had the pleasure of not only experiencing this unique and compelling story of what it took for us to survive as a new business and thrive as it matured to adulthood, but I had a hand in guiding the various stages of its evolution. I believe my behind-the-scenes vantage point, covering almost the entire history of the company, can provide education for businesses that are at various stages of maturity and convey the personal story of a business that so many people contributed to along its road to success. This is the adventure of Wright Express, now known as WEX, and its winding, precarious road to WEXcellence. And it's an adventure I would now like to share with you.

Chapter 1

Walk the Line: The Journey Begins

There are those gifted with an ability to develop a unique business concept. A gifted leader can mold that concept like clay into a viable business model.

THE FOUNDATION OF A BUSINESS

Various studies show that within five years, over 50 percent of startup businesses fail and are no longer in business. By year twelve, a much smaller percentage has survived. Some have gone out of business, while others have been sold to, or absorbed by, larger companies. The statistics do not even reveal how well those that have survived on their own are doing. The point is that very few startups go on to achieve profitability, much less become success stories.

In light of these mortality rates, it's easy to understand that the early years are more about surviving than thriving. Businesses are looking to stay afloat while they lay the foundations for their future. What can make this more challenging is when a business engages with venture capital (VC) funders. This adds an entirely new dimension to these startups by raising the stakes on what success is supposed to look like and how soon it should be achieved. For the VCs, it's about more than just survival; achievement requires ratcheted growth and high levels of success and returns to keep these funders happy.

Wright Express eventually engaged with venture capitalists who would remain in the mix for a long time, although some would back out and be replaced by others once the business required more capital. Thanks largely to the VCs, the company would manage to sustain for nearly a decade before showing a profit in 1993. It was a rocky road, to say the least, and one that I became part of in 1986, less than a year after VC funding began, which was still during the company's infancy.

Wright Express was actually formed in 1983 as a new business venture for A.R. Wright Co., a family-owned and run company based in Portland, Maine, that provided home-heating oil. A.R. Wright Co. was a mainstay in the area with roots dating back to 1895.

It was a young man named Parker Poole III, a Tufts University engineering graduate, and part of a new generation of family leaders, who wanted to make his mark, so he turned to the Wright family in hopes of creating a new chapter in the family's ongoing legacy. In the early 1980s, Poole foresaw the emergence of electronic banking and recognized that it could potentially be adapted into an unattended electronic-vehicle fueling business, targeted primarily at companies with vehicles or fleets. He met with his uncle, Bill Richardson, then president and chairman of A.R. Wright Co., along with the board of directors, and convinced them to provide seed money for the new venture. Using the seed money, Poole began laying the foundation for the aptly named Wright Express before the business launched in 1983.

Building the foundation of a business typically starts with creating and then validating an innovative business model designed to successfully forge a new path in a specific market. It requires persistence and determination, and should VC expectations be added to the mix, it requires some big, bold goals. Leaders must be committed, since the VCs will not accept anything short of strong, clear methods for building the pathways to success, methods that should also generate enthusiasm from those who come on board.

Along with a strong business model, the young Wright Express, or WEX, had a few key factors that brought most of the management team on board. In fact, all but one of the original management team came from outside the state. Only the CFO was a local hire. He was a rather established finance leader working for the Maine offices of Guy Gannet Company, the newspaper giant founded in 1906.

While the business plan was a strong selling point, the majority of us were also seduced by the state of Maine. In real estate, they use the old adage "location, location, location." Clearly it can also be appropriate in business, as the location certainly played a role in bringing most of us to WEX. Maine is not very populated, but when people get here, they fall in love with the quality of life and the calm, safe environment tucked away in the sheer beauty of the state. People simply don't want to leave.

In fact, a recent poll, taken nationwide, asked people if they had a chance to leave their state would they want to do so. Maine was voted one of the most loyal states in the nation. However, this positive view of Maine, and especially Portland, wasn't always the case. I remember Parker commenting to me back in the mid-1980s that the Portland area had not experienced any sort of renaissance since the Great Depression and the town and area were not very appealing. But finally, by the late 1980s the city and area were enjoying an awakening, with companies like L.L.Bean, UNUM, National Semiconductor, IDEXX, WEX, Hannaford, Cole Haan, and Fairchild growing and adding to the business fabric and bringing good-paying jobs and career opportunities for its citizens.

As a result, the people who made the life transition to Maine wanted to stay put and were willing to work very hard in order to do so. Unlike startups in New York City or Silicon Valley, where there are numerous choices, and many employees come in with one foot already out the door, Maine has far fewer startups, so we had a much greater incentive to make this business work. I think the fact that the Wright family was respected and a mainstay in the area also helped bring us in, along with stock options and the idea of being in on the ground floor of something that we all believed could potentially pay off handsomely and help us all stay in Maine.

Laying the foundation for a startup, beyond having innovative ideas and a solid business model, is largely about finding people who are committed, passionate, entrepreneurial, invested, and persistent about the mission and are willing to do whatever it takes to succeed. For WEX, everyone had a role and it didn't matter what they had done in a prior life, here you had to be all in. It is important to find people who are willing to roll up their sleeves to get things done, and this defined the folks at WEX. Everyone had to work closely with their people in each particular discipline, whether it was finance, marketing, IT, or operations.

Another key aspect of laying a strong foundation is hiring people who get along with one another. Startups require working very long hours. We were putting in seventy-five to eighty-five hour weeks. It's easy to find a common bond when you are all working hard and sharing a commitment. We would have parties and have families over to each other's homes for the holidays. It became a family bonding experience because of the sheer amount of work, and WEX became our social fabric. We began to call ourselves WEXers, and in a sense, it was a lot like being part of a group of close friends who spend so much formative time together that it sets the foundation for a lot of what will happen later in your life. In fact, our early bonding as a management team remained so strong that, over the years, six presidents came and went, but many of us stayed together, and it was all because of those early days of rolling our sleeves up and working seventy-five hours a week to fulfill a vision.

It is also extremely important that you start a new business with people who are able to pivot, if and when necessary. We shared a culture built on finding a way to make things work even if we needed to go back and rethink specific ideas or goals. Despite the best-laid plans and the most finely tuned business model, startups learn (and grow) a lot from trial and error. There are times when you simply have to throw something at the wall and see if it sticks, and if it doesn't you need to pivot and try again. In 1986, we had to do a major pivot, realizing that the franchise program, with which we started out, was not going to work. The money invested in the original business plan was washed down the drain and we "rebooted" from square one. We'll talk more about our second beginning of WEX in Chapter 3, Infancy 2.0. The point is, what made such a major restart work was that all of us onboard were able to pivot. We had the kind of flexibility that is imperative at the start of a new business. People who are married to their initial ideas or who will take their ball and go home if things are not going as planned, typically will not last long in a startup.

CHARACTER AND INSTITUTIONAL MEMORY—CULTURAL INFLUENCES

Assuming a company makes it, these formative years are the foundation for the character that is developed during the ultimately successful childhood and adolescent stages, and eventually, the adult or more mature business stage.

This character foundation will become even more ingrained if there is institutional memory provided by executive leaders who have persevered through the various stages of development; in other words, the people who, from the very beginning, helped forge this evolving character development. But leadership longevity is rare in today's businesses, and this presents certain problems. If too much management turnover occurs, and leadership roles are subsequently filled from the outside, long-term memory is obscured and may be compromised. Although the character foundation may be present, it is not appreciated or valued as it should be.

New management often recognizes, "I have this company, I have this product, I have these relationships, I have these people, I have this culture," and then shifts to, "So what am I going to do now to make my own imprint?" They don't relate inherently to that institutional memory, for obvious reasons. They might hear about the company's history—the highs and lows, and all the dramatic fluctuations along the way—and have a general sense of what it took to get the business to this point, but they're not emotionally invested because they didn't live it.

15

In some business models, memory retention may not be as important, especially if the business has gone through difficult stages of change. But for WEX, strategic partnerships have defined our platform for success. The institutional memory of WEX enhanced our success and sustainability, and we have seized every opportunity to honor the fundamental cultural distinctions that have helped us shape our business personality in a positive, impactful way.

It is, therefore, very significant to build a foundation with the hopes of keeping employees on board for the long term. While there is never a guarantee, you want to find people who are passionate about what you do and how you do it. This is because the core attribute of any brand is the emotional investment people within it and/or its customers make in that business —the deeper the investment, the more enduring the relationship. For me personally, I was committed to working hard to establish and grow my career, but WEX also offered up an opportunity for me to be creative and innovative in an uncharted business space, and that was unexpected, but so very energizing and inspiring. I believe my passion and vision helped me find believers who wanted to be part of the story for their own vested interests and for the good of the team and the company. My drive to forge enduring partnerships paved the way for symbiotic long-term relationships, built on increasing value and trust.

HOW WE DID THINGS

Every time we could demonstrate the advantages inherent in doing business with WEX, every time we had the opportunity to represent the integrity of WEX, every time we could build more loyal relationships, we jumped on it. That was all part of how we were building a long-term, sustainable business model. Over time we built and utilized our culture as a strategic advantage in our business model. That's what distinguished WEX.

"How we did things" was ingrained early on in our culture. It reflected what first impressed me about the people of Maine: if you treat them fairly and build a two-way street—when you're being honest, transparent, and fair—they will embrace the vision, work hard to realize it, and be loyal to the cause. We treated the Mainers with great respect, especially since so many of us were new to their beautiful corner of the world. As a result, they accepted us and gave us their all. Early on, everyone was excited to be part of something new and innovative; it was the common driver that made us all passionate about finding the pathways to success. No one was making a lot of money, we couldn't offer much security, and the pitfalls were numerous. Nevertheless, people were excited about finding the path to success. They were, and still are, loyal, hardworking, persistent, and compassionate people who take great pride in their work.

I come from a background where you don't mislead people, you don't lie, and you don't deceive. Perhaps you can't tell everybody everything all the time because you can't let certain things leak out prematurely. But you also never misrepresent, mislead, or act in a dishonest manner. You strive for honesty and transparency, so people are not faced with surprises. While you're not perfect, you always tell your associates and partners when you make a mistake and you then do everything in your power to fix it. You build their trust by letting them see that you mean what you say and say what you mean, and that you're going to make it work.

This philosophy permeated how WEX built its value proposition for customers and partners. It was the foundation for how we treated our people, creating an energy that became contagious. Together we all bought into the two-way street and established the foundation of our culture that would eventually define WEX in a meaningful way. We were building something special, brick by brick. And that's what is so engaging about the story of WEX.

INFANCY (1983–1986)

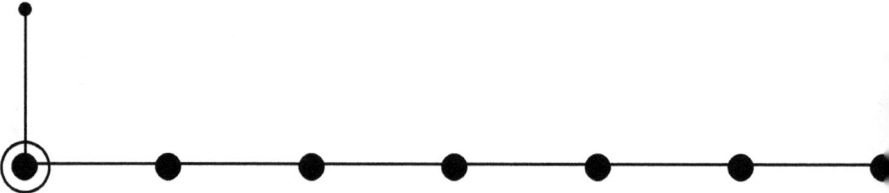

20

Chapter 2

A Pivot Toward a Bold, New Vision

Infancy is a time during which the basic foundation is built. Early in this stage of development, exploration and risks are taken, from which learning occurs; a behavior modification or change of course sometimes becomes necessary.

In the early infancy years, some aspects of the business become more perfunctory—many aspects of the business may not be fully developed yet, but they are merely a means to an end. During this infancy stage, the company's goal is to mature and stand on its own. It is so driven and narrowly focused on establishing itself as a functioning organization that there is no room to worry about complete balance. As a result, the company may sacrifice some level of benevolence with its people, as well as the community. During this time, the basic capabilities of the company must be proven or the company can compromise its ability to raise additional funding and survive.

At some point, it is important to work toward and manage a properly balanced portfolio, but some business components may have to be compromised early on, until the business is a true "going concern." This is the basic nature of startups in their infancy stage. This reality may be difficult for management and for the associates to embrace, but the energy of the organization is more directed toward fulfilling a new and bold vision.

THE INITIAL VISION

Every business starts with an idea, some of which are better than others, but sometimes the most fruitful ideas grow into something sustainable.

Parker Poole's vision was to fully develop unattended electronic-fueling stations for fleets where a driver would use a card to authorize and activate a fueling pump. This was not incrementalism, it was revolutionary in trying to insert an innovation well before its time. Parker perfected the idea by partnering with NCR Corporation, an established company with electronic retail terminals or Point of Sale (POS) terminals. Together they concluded that such technology could be reconfigured for fuel-pump authorization. His business model was mobilized in the greater Portland area through a network of four fueling locations that fleets could access throughout their routes.

Essentially, what Poole did was take the NCR POS machine that was originally built to allow electronic retailing and reconfigure it on a fueling island to allow the automated dispensing of fuel with the use of a charge card. The electronic POS terminal could be used to connect to all the gasoline and diesel pumps on a fuel island, and once an authorization was completed, dispense the appropriate product.

It would work like this: the driver would enter the station, insert the WEX card, and select which pump to authorize. The POS machine would read the magnetic strip on the card embedded with the account and the vehicle identification numbers. It would then instantaneously check the fleet's credit to see if the fleet was in good standing and to see if the vehicle number was valid for that particular fleet. Before the pump turned on, the driver would have to key in his or her own personal driver ID (this was similar to a pin number, but was unrelated to the vehicle itself, as any driver could drive any vehicle, as long as they had the card that identified that vehicle). If the account, vehicle, and driver numbers were all authorized, the pump would turn on and enable fueling of the vehicle.

In this Portland market microcosm, the new system succeeded in attracting and retaining businesses. But Poole did not stop there. His business model called for franchising the idea and selling exclusive territories to independent petroleum companies in the United States so that these companies could develop their own fueling networks in their exclusive territories. The premise was that a WEX card would be used to activate the fueling transaction and could be used by the fleet signed by a franchisee to buy fuel in the franchisee's exclusive territory, as well as at other participating franchised territories. This would effectively create a broader network for fleets of all sizes to take advantage of this network of fueling stops. The franchisee who signed the fleet would bill its fleets, regardless of where they fueled in the network. The franchisee would pay a fee to other franchisees if the fleet had purchased fuel at another franchisee's fueling location. This created a win for the fleet to have a broader network of fueling locations and a win for all franchisees to realize sales to fleets they hadn't signed themselves.

In addition to authorizing the transaction, the other selling point was that the software captured valuable data, including the vehicle's and driver's identification, the time and date of transaction, the location, product, quantity, price, and odometer reading. The fleet operator could review every transaction for every vehicle and know which driver made a purchase, what they bought, at what time, on what date, and where. Was it premium unleaded gas and was that allowed by the fleet? If so, how many gallons?

WEX provided all of those answers to the fleet manager through a descriptive monthly paper report. The capabilities on the front end at the point of sale and through the reports would eliminate most, if not all, of the unauthorized purchases and guesswork of who was authorized to fuel and who was not. With more experience and verification, we could eventually make the claim that the fleets could save 5 to 15 percent on their gasoline and diesel purchases by using the program, all because of the data, tracking, and security that was enabled within the cards.

WEX also had the ability to implement security features on the cards, such as restricting the card to fuel-only. In the future, the card could be utilized at pump locations where other vehicle and non-vehicle items were also available to purchase. Therefore, if a driver tried to buy, as we would say, "smokes and cokes" with a WEX card, they were barred from doing so. If they came into the store and said, "I just purchased fifteen gallons of gasoline, and I'd like to add a Coke to my purchase," when the attendant tried to punch in the merchandise code for soda, it would be rejected.

We put a similar security measure in place in a number of other circumstances. If, for example, a driver was laid off but kept the WEX card and still tried to make a personal purchase using the card, the transaction would be declined, assuming the fleet manager had called to shut off the card or the driver ID, knowing the driver was being laid off. In another scenario, if a driver had filled up the company vehicle and then filled up their personal vehicle on the WEX card, the information report sent to the business office could highlight this unauthorized purchase if the total gallons exceeded the vehicle's tank capacity.

25

Parker's idea was innovative in that it would both capture electronically at the pump what was charged on the card and all the other related information mentioned above, at the time of the fueling transaction. However, at that time, when anyone went into a gas station, all credit card transactions were captured manually through an imprinter (zip-zap machine) inside the station, not at the pump.

The primary information captured manually was the date, dollar amount, perhaps the product purchased, and the address of the gas station that was already embedded in the imprinter device. Even for fleets, they likely had a simplified paper-based fleet card from one of the oil companies, and when a driver handed it to an attendant during fueling, the paper receipts would get authorized, be accumulated for a couple of days, and then sent off by mail to a processing center. The processing center had people who would then manually enter information from the ticket (the product and dollar amount). All in all, it was a slow, ineffective, possibly inaccurate, and soon to be outmoded process.

Parker's inventive approach was certainly ahead of its time, since pay-at-the-pump credit card capabilities did not take root until the mid-1990s, when Mobil became a strong adopter of the technology and began to roll it out en masse at their stations. However, when Parker was attempting to build a network of stand-alone electronic unattended fueling stations in the early- to mid-1980s, the petroleum industry was still trying to figure out how to make a smooth transition from paper to electronic fueling transactions.

Parker had the proprietary software and NCR had the unattended authorization systems. A petroleum marketer would buy rights to a territory, purchase the packaged software and hardware solution, and pay a franchise fee for every fleet card transaction enabled. It was the perfect cocktail to enable electronic transactions nationwide... or so it seemed.

To make this franchising plan work, WEX would require capital funding beyond the family's capability. There would be significant costs to enable the marketing and management of the franchise program; to develop the mainframe solution to capture, report, and bill purchases for the franchisees; and to support the systems used by the petroleum marketers to authorize and manage their programs. On the surface, the ingredients for success seemed reasonable.

The family and WEX sought out additional VC funding and raised their first venture capital round in the fall of 1985, in addition to their own participation in the funding of this new enterprise. The venture capital companies also insisted on hiring industry experts and talent to manage and steward their investment.

A local, experienced CFO was brought in, as well as a microprocessor expert, a mainframe authorization expert, and a credit card expert. This highly specialized team was assembled to drive the business model to success and secure a return for the VCs. Keep in mind that all VC-backed startups have a little bit of the "burning platform" syndrome, wherein survival is expected, but VC patience is limited. To expedite the marketing progress, in late 1985, the VCs believed Parker should also hire a marketing executive, ideally someone with petroleum experience, to market and sell the franchises.

And that's where I come in.

I was hired in January of 1986, shortly after the VCs made their initial investment in WEX. I would proceed to experience nine years of VC ownership where success was not only in question, but the initial business model was scrapped and we essentially started over with a new one. In my eighth year, we finally turned a profit, but by then many of the VCs were tired, scared, and/or frustrated. We were sold to SafeCard in 1994. Over the next seven years, WEX would find itself owned by five parent companies. There were times when the management would have liked to purchase the company through a management buyout (MBO), but for various reasons, such a buyout never materialized. Finally, in 2005, we were jettisoned by our then-parent company into the public marketplace through an initial public offering (IPO).

But I'm getting way ahead of myself.

MEET MIKE DUBYAK

Prior to joining WEX, I had been working in the petroleum industry for over a decade (1974–1985), ever since I graduated from college. I began my career at Pennzoil in Cleveland and then relocated to their corporate offices in Houston. While in Houston, a good friend of mine, working in human resources, suggested that I take a personal values-based evaluation assessment, which gave me some insight into what I wanted to focus on in my life. The results of the assessment suggested that if I could get into something entrepreneurial, it would satisfy my personal goals and values.

Consequently, I left Pennzoil to take a job in 1977 with a startup in Pittsburgh, composed of only the founder (a former executive at Ashland Oil), his wife, and a secretary. We had big dreams of selling petroleum fuels, heavy fuels, motor oils, and asphalt into the commercial market, made up of steel mills, industrial plants, coal companies, and trucking companies. Together we fulfilled that dream. The company became quite successful, growing to over 150 people. By the early 1980s, we were supplying petroleum products in approximately eight states by barge, trains, trucks, pipelines, and packages.

However, as the industrial base in these states, especially in western Pennsylvania, started to contract, we faced downsizing. As a young man, I concluded that I didn't want to continue pursuing my career in a contracting and less dynamic market. Because of these circumstances, I also concluded that I didn't necessarily want to stay in Pittsburgh. When I left the company in 1985, the 150 people had been cut back to roughly 50.

During a vacation to Cape Cod in 1982, I traveled along the northern New England coast and fell in love with the people and the natural beauty of the region. Even though I had no job and we did not know anyone in the area, I eventually rolled the dice and made the bold move with my wife and one-and-a-half-year-old daughter to the Portsmouth, New Hampshire area in August 1985. My goal was to network and find a new career in a location somewhere between Boston, Massachusetts and Portland, Maine. Keep in mind that the oil industry at this time was in a downturn, and many people were losing their jobs. Little did I know at this juncture of my life that I was about to embark upon a journey that would ultimately change everything for me.

Through contacts, I received the names of various Maine-based petroleum companies, one of which was A.R. Wright. I was given the name of Harvey Patry in Portland, and it was to Harvey that I addressed my marketing letter (Harvey had sold his business to A.R. Wright Co. and was now employed by them). I stated in the letter that I had a background in the petroleum industry and explained the work that I had done in Cleveland, Houston, and Pittsburgh, which included commercial fuel and oil sales, as well as the marketing experience I already had under my belt. In my letter, I was asking Harvey if he knew of anyone within the region in the petroleum industry that might be interested in my experience and capabilities.

As Harvey would later tell the story, he opened my letter and quickly disposed of it in the wastebasket. Later that day, Parker was talking to Harvey and he conveyed that the VCs were intent on him hiring a petroleum marketing executive. He asked Harvey if he knew anyone who would fit the bill, and Harvey said, "No, I don't." But he then recalled the letter and reached under his desk and pulled out his wastebasket. After a few moments of sifting through trash, he found the letter and handed it to Parker.

"I just received this letter earlier today," he explained.

We all need a little luck in life, and this fateful development helped shape not only my career—but my life. There was no headhunter involved and no formal search process; it was all just blind luck that my letter found its way into the hands of Parker Poole III in Portland, Maine on that day. A few hours later, the wastebasket would have been emptied and I would have lost out on the opportunity of a lifetime—the opportunity to pursue this new business venture.

I was invited to Portland for an interview and realized an opportunity existed in a completely new endeavor I had not yet heard of, called Wright Express (WEX), and not in the A.R. Wright home-heating oil business. During the negotiation process, it became apparent that I would not be receiving the perks I enjoyed in Pittsburgh, and I would have a base salary that was two-thirds of what I was previously earning. However, I would receive stock options in this exciting new startup that fit the goals I had set for myself since early on. I made the decision that my personal and professional success would be based on hard work and my desire to be part of an entrepreneurial opportunity. I also knew that I wanted, at some point, to have ownership in the company where I applied that hard work.

In January of 1986, I started work at WEX, where I would head up marketing and sales. So there I was, committed to this opportunity in a place I wanted to live, with a startup where I could utilize my prior work experience and where my entrepreneurial passion was satisfied. It was an exciting time in the business and an exciting time in my career. I was prepared to work hard to help realize the vision I was buying into, albeit at a substantial salary decrease, because I was willing to bet on a future. I was committed to the vision and would do whatever it took to make it come to fruition.

I felt lucky, fortunate, and committed. What they got was not so much a sales or marketing professional, but a person who needed to believe in something so much that growing the company into a success story became a personal cause. I pursued it with complete passion and perseverance.

Finding a cause had always been important to me. I grew up in a steel mill town, Struthers, Ohio, which was near Youngstown, a hardworking, lower-middle-class area that was primarily blue-collar. Growing up in this environment instilled great work and personal values in me, from early on. My mother was someone who sized up everybody based on his or her own merits, and I learned a lot from her. She was perhaps the biggest influence when it came to shaping my values. My father died when I was ten years old. He was an entrepreneur and that may have rubbed off on me even at a young age. He went through his own trials and tribulations, and as I grew older I began to understand more about what he had gone through. We all go through tough times, but unfortunately for me, his tough time took place while I was growing up. Before my father's passing, the rest of my at-home family—my mother, my sister, and I—endured some financial troubles and this weighed heavily on my mother's shoulders. I saw the effect it had on all of us, and it left me with fear, realizing how vulnerable and fragile life can be.

After my father died, I came to realize that I never wanted to be a burden to my mother or do anything in my life that would give her reason to worry about me or cause trouble for her. I often felt like I had to be the rock back then, the "man" in the family. As a result of this, I grew up fast and lost some of my childhood. But I kept this all to myself. I never shared these feelings with anyone. From an early age, I was a serious young man who was incredibly driven and who had the ability to take on responsibility and make decisions. We all react to life-changing events differently. I consider them defining moments. These events impact us in such profound ways and they create who we become. This was my defining moment.

Perhaps growing up within this family dynamic helped contribute in some way to me being an introvert. One of the characteristics of an introvert is that they work very hard to get things right, and they don't need or rely upon outside influencers to help make decisions. They also go back and reflect for a while before coming up with an answer, especially if it's a complex question or problem.

In an August 24, 2015 *Wall Street Journal* article by Elizabeth Bernstein, "Why Introverts Make Great Entrepreneurs," she outlines some of the traits common to most introverts that make them especially well-suited for entrepreneurship. One trait that's cited in the article that I've always particularly identified with is that entrepreneurs "tend to rely on their own inner compass, rather than relying on external signals when determining that they are making the right move or doing a good job."

Being an introvert stemmed from my childhood, but it has actually given me an edge throughout my career and life. It has allowed me to depend on my own instincts, think things through, and then move on to see the big picture and make decisions largely free of outside influences.

A lot has also been written about intrinsic and extrinsic motivation, which follows in line with introverts and extroverts. If you are intrinsically motivated, you seek self-validation rather than being motivated to succeed because of what others will say and the awards and acclaim you may receive. I've never found myself seeking the praise of others but instead have always been my own toughest critic. It's how I feel inside about what I do and who I am that has always motivated me.

Another significant part of my youth was sports. I played varsity basketball in high school and during all four years in college and captained both teams, which was another experience that I chalk up to playing an important role in guiding me to become the person I am today. It not only gave me discipline and taught me what it was like to be part of a team, but it created leadership opportunities for me and reemphasized my mother's beliefs on how to treat other people.

What I took away from those years, and what they instilled in me today, was never to judge anyone based on their size, their height, their gender, where they come from, or the color of their skin. In my view, everybody on the court in any game was to be judged only on his or her own merits. And that is how I've always gone through my life—by accepting people based on their values—not on their looks, position, or résumé.

My values ran deep then and still do today.

So, when I was presented with this new opportunity to join WEX, I knew it was going to be more than just a job. I had found my cause to pursue and a team on which to pursue it. I was all in and completely committed.

THE FATAL FLAW

So why is WEX not a franchise program today? The product worked, the local fleets embraced it, the market was ripe for innovation, and there was a huge market. What was the problem?

Every electronic system configuration offered by WEX/NCR cost approximately $30,000 to install for each retail location, while the competing product configurations available were roughly half this price, ranging from $12,000 to $15,000. NCR may have had a superior product for most retailing industries, but its functionality for the fleet-fueling petroleum industry did not allow for the price differential.

Believe it or not, the oil companies' profits, in terms of the margins they make at the pump, are much like the profits in the grocery store business: you have to sell a lot (of gallons) to make a little bit of profit. You're likely making a few cents on every gallon you're selling, depending on what part of the retail supply chain you're in. Parker, NCR, and the VCs did not fully appreciate that petroleum marketers typically made such a small margin on fuel. Consequently, return on investment was challenging, especially at the higher price point for the WEX/NCR option.

The entire value proposition was a huge financial commitment for an independent petroleum marketer. Owning an exclusive territory and populating it with multiple, stand-alone, and expensive unattended electronic-fueling sites proved challenging. It just wasn't feasible or cost effective. NCR primarily wanted to supply their high-end machines because they thought convenience-store operators who were selling merchandise inside would put in one of their electronic cash registers that could not only control the pump (with all the data we wanted to capture) but would also control all their inventory management inside the store as well. They anticipated that this would provide the capabilities to read the bar scans on merchandise that was sold as well as controlling fuel sales and inventory. For NCR, this was an opportunity to sell their high-end microprocessor cash registers. For Wright Express, the fleet-fueling proposition and the product represented just one ancillary product solution enabled by the NCR electronic cash register product.

Even if a petroleum marketer bought into the opportunity, the best-case scenario would have been the ability for them to install a few automated fueling sites at a time. This would have restricted the number of convenient locations accepting the new card. Because of this I, as well as others, became convinced that NCR and WEX would not be successful in selling an expensive product and signing a sufficient number of franchisees to make it worthwhile for the VCs. I began to read the writing on the wall.

Ultimately, the VCs realized the proprietary electronic software sales would be slow, meaning fuel volume sales would be minimal. This meant slow adoption and slow growth, which would limit revenues for WEX and could easily result in the VCs' reluctance to continue investing, and eventually having them write us off completely.

SALVAGE AND RECONFIGURATIONS

The business model WEX and NCR envisioned and the VCs invested in would not lead to a successful ending for the VCs, the family, or the company management. It was time to make the pivot mentioned earlier. It was time to smash the clay of this failed vision flat on the table and start over from scratch. This was clearly a huge risk, but the alternative was fatal!

Together with others, I was instrumental in introducing a life-changing and life-saving pivot by bringing forward a new and radical change to the business model. Given my background in the oil industry, I understood the independent petroleum marketers' economic business model, which included petroleum industry pricing dynamics and margin sensitivities embedded in the retail-fueling environment. It was also clear that fleets required convenience in locating participating fleet card acceptance sites if they were to sign on to use the fleet card.

What was also happening at that time in the petroleum industry was that oil companies were figuring out how to adopt electronic authorization and data capture solutions on their own and they were also starting to focus on the use of smaller, in-store devices. These devices would read data off of a card's magnetic strip, and that information would be sent off for authorization instantly. Additionally, these devices did not cost $30,000 installed as ours would have cost. At the time, they probably cost between $1,000 and $1,500 apiece. They didn't authorize directly at the pump, instead they were in the store or a kiosk behind the counter.

The oil companies were making the decision to put these electronic solutions at most, if not all their gas stations because they wanted to move away from capturing card transactions with the older zip-zap model where, eventually, a person in a processing center would be keying in limited data about the transaction. We saw this trend developing in the retail petroleum industry, and we knew that if we wanted to stay ahead of the emerging trend, we would have to make a drastic change to our business model ASAP.

The pivot called for salvaging the true value-add of the product, which was the security and control of the tracking information captured at the point of sale. If we could retain this value-add security and control product, and then package it with the payment capability of a charge card, we could then market it to larger petroleum companies that were now getting ready to deploy their less complex and less expensive electronic terminals to capture their proprietary oil company cards, as well as Amex, Visa, and MasterCard.

We would now turn our focus to convincing these larger petroleum marketers to build in our WEX cards' electronic point-of-sale specification to capture our data and security features that were so valuable to fleets. If successful, we would get mass acceptance at thousands of locations for each oil company agreeing to buy into our program. This would provide much larger-scale acceptance versus a slow rollout by franchisees of the automated pay-at-the-pump configuration in the former model.

We became convinced that fleets required convenience of location, which meant we needed to create a larger footprint of fueling sites where the fleet card would be accepted. Pivoting to this strategy would mean that the unattended fueling stations and franchise model would be abandoned.

This was a bold move and would require first getting Parker and the family to buy in, then the rest of management team, and finally the VCs who had invested their money on a very different business model. The reality was that a good portion of the money already invested was going to be flushed down the drain with the original failed business model. We knew this, even if they didn't know it yet. The question for the VCs was really: would they want to continue funding this new business model?

Ultimately, we won over enough support to move forward under this completely different business model, albeit sustaining significant collateral damage. Once we presented our new vision to the VCs and some of them agreed to the new business model, I was nominated to address NCR at their

Dallas sales meeting in 1986. I was tasked with delivering the news of our change of course, which resulted in fireworks with this strategic partner.

The NCR sales meeting would turn out to be one of the historical events that changed the course of our future. It served as a platform for NCR to talk to its sales force about the great capabilities and updates for its microprocessor cash register, which could satisfy many management needs in the convenience store environment. At this meeting, what NCR expected was that I was going to stand up, address its sales force team, and explain how our fleet card would integrate with their devices and create additional value for their sales pitch to oil companies. But that wasn't exactly what I was going to say.

The VCs wanted the news about our change of direction to come from me because, after all, I was the petroleum expert at WEX and it would be difficult for Parker to deliver the news. They wanted me to explain why I thought it was the only way our fleet card program could be successful. I didn't sleep at all the night before the meeting, because I knew the task I was being sent there to do might not be well received.

So, the next day at the meeting, I did it. I stood up and addressed the sales organization, which included executives who were advocates and supporters of the NCR/WEX business model, telling them we didn't believe that we could sell the fleet card effectively without having other, smaller, low-cost devices to supplement the NCR sophisticated option, given what we were seeing in the marketplace. In a nutshell, I was essentially saying to NCR, "If you won't supply these other devices, then we need to go to another equipment provider that will supply them." But the reality was that those devices were not in their product set and they were intent on selling their more sophisticated, value-based, high-end electronic cash registers and POS machines. The NCR executives immediately pulled Parker into a conference room and I left the meeting.

It was at this moment that everything went crazy. My presentation lit the match and things started burning, fast. By 1987, we no longer had any affiliation with NCR.

Instead of WEX becoming a statistic supporting the high mortality rate of startups, we provided a new vision and the opportunity to succeed, but under a very different, very innovative business model.

This new and radical vision did have its casualties, which played out over the next few years. It led to the founder, Parker Poole III, eventually leaving the company. It also led to no reasonable return on the family's investment in the venture. They cashed in their chips and basically just got their money back. It also led to a shake-up of some key management, whose skills were no longer relevant to the new model. To top it off, many VCs were losing patience and not willing to continue investing in this new model, and a whole host of new VC firms were entering to take their place as investors, adding to the mayhem as this brave new endeavor began.

We were like an infant, screaming and squirming, trying to find and get our way. WEX wasn't just finding its footing; we were learning to stand, and hopefully walk, in a whole new world. We had a bold new vision, and we'd need brave new strategies to bring it all to fruition.

The pivot was painful, but it was indispensable. Our new course or our rebirth, so to speak, came with a bold vision, and along the way, this bold but articulated vision helped convince VCs to fund us, enticed oil companies and fleets to want to be part of our vision, and attracted talented people to buy in by aligning their careers with WEX. By believing so strongly in this business model, my passion was ever-present and influenced various stakeholders to also believe and invest in various ways. Yet, all of this would unfold over time. WEX would embrace the new business model and start anew in 1987. Once again, we would roll up our sleeves as we launched into our second infancy stage.

INFANCY 2.0 (1986–1990)

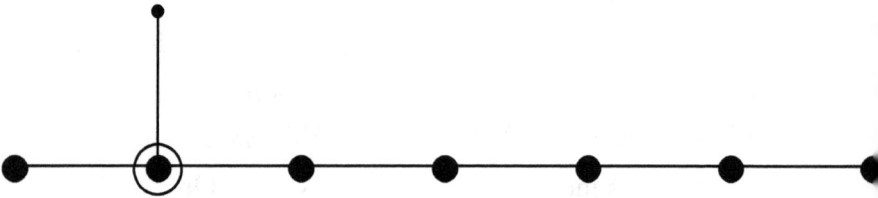

Chapter 3

Cracking the Chicken-or-Egg

Failure to crack this conundrum meant we would become a startup who had a failed vision...and become just another statistic.

We had definitely created a better business model, but we now faced a conundrum, which involved the classic chicken-or-egg dilemma.

First, why would a petroleum marketer sign on to integrate and accept our fleet card product at all their retail fueling sites when we had no fleets signed on to use our fleet card? And second, why would a fleet agree to use our fleet card when there were no fuel sites accepting the card?

We had to resolve this. Unfortunately, we had already spent millions of dollars on a failed business model. We were painfully aware of this. Now we had a new model that still had its own fundamental hurdles to overcome.

I've heard it said that you don't see someone's true colors when times are good or the going is easy. It's only in the midst of challenges and obstacles that we find out what we are truly made of. That was certainly true of our company. We had a colossal chicken-or-egg problem on our hands, and one of our first critical success factors became finding the path to solving it. Our future clearly depended on it. If we didn't crack this dilemma we were done. We had already started over with some VCs staying on board while others eventually dropped out. We had brought in some new VCs, but we knew that there was no room for failure at this point.

PHYSICAL BEING: CORE FLEET PRODUCT VALUE

The core product that ultimately defined the value of WEX in the respective market was the security and control measures provided by our fleet card product. We provided fleet owners and managers with robust data that could save them 5 to 15 percent on driver and vehicle expenses. We provided robust authorization features and data collection at the point of sale. Today, WEX has this type of embedded software included in more than 90 percent of the approximate 150,000 retail fueling locations in the United States, where it captures the account, vehicle, and driver identification. All three have to be authorized before the pump will turn on to allow the driver to pump the fuel. At the time, it was an innovative security and control value proposition. Not only were there three levels of authorization necessary for the driver to buy fuel, but the WEX software embedded at each accepting fueling site would retrieve the location, date, and time of the transaction, plus capturing the quantity, price per gallon, and vehicle odometer reading.

This allowed the fleet owners and managers to put limits on driver purchases. They were able to monitor data in a way that was not possible with other available card products. We could sit down with a fleet manager and ask how many vehicles they had and what restrictions they wanted on driver purchases. All of this would be managed and customized by authorized personnel. Eventually it was managed through an easy-to-use online system available to the fleet. From the very beginning, the product was clearly a precision-based, value-add product strategy, where the greatest values offered to the fleet were the security, control, and information services.

At the beginning, this win-win situation was not a shoo-in for success. We had the best new innovative solution, but no acceptance. There were multiple competitive payment alternatives available to the fleets, but we didn't have acceptance at petroleum sites and had not yet proven ourselves. The other payment alternatives did not possess the value-add of the security and control features we had built into our product, but they did offer convenience of location. The alternative to our card, which was a general-purpose credit card, had full acceptance at all petroleum brands, or in the case of a proprietary oil card, acceptance at all the company's branded retail sites. For WEX, the acceptance of our card was the critical success factor. Without acceptance, our business model was jeopardized. After all, who wants to carry a card if no one accepts it?

We saw this as an opportunity. If we could embed our innovative product and system at a sufficient number of fueling sites, we believed we could revolutionize the fleet-fueling market. We knew fleets would love our product—we just had to deliver the site acceptance to them, meaning we had to get the oil companies on board.

Once we could deliver the convenience of sufficient fueling sites, we could build and deploy a go-to-market strategy, marketing this system to the vast network of fleets by getting them to realize the savings they could enjoy by using our fleet card product. The rest, as they say, would be history.

THE TARGET MARKET

The United States, at that time, had more than six million fleets composed of more than forty million vehicles. We saw that as an enormous opportunity and knew that every one of those vehicles needed fuel, to the tune of more than eighty billion gallons per year. Keep in mind this includes all types of vehicles: automobiles, vans, and light, medium, and heavy trucks. Even more interesting was the fact that over thirty-five million of those forty million commercial vehicles were part of fleets with less than thirty vehicles, or basically small businesses.

Overall, it was, and still is, a huge, diverse, and fragmented market covering various business classifications and government agencies. The target market for WEX would be the fleets fueling at retail sites. We were targeting the vans and light trucks at those sites, not at truck stops where the tractor-trailer fleets purchase fuel.

We knew there was a huge fleet market with a real need, but we were still in a quandary. How would we crack the code to get our product accepted by the oil companies? We needed our card to be accepted at a sufficient number of fueling sites to make it attractive to the fleets.

Keep in mind that back in the 1980s, the largest retail oil company was Texaco, with around 15,000 locations: approximately 10 percent of the retail fuel site market. Most of the other major oil companies had approximately 12,000 locations each, and the top ten oil companies accounted for approximately 55 percent of all the retail fuel locations in the US. The other 45 percent were controlled by regional mid majors and independently branded retail marketers.

Our goal was to have the oil companies build in our specification, which was more complex than that of the other cards they accepted. In addition, our pricing to the oil companies was targeted at the highest level of any credit or charge card they accepted. On the surface those factors by themselves were a hard nut to crack. This was compounded by the fact that we had no customers (outside of a few thousand in the greater Portland area). In addition, the fleets across the country were already buying from the oil companies either by using cash, general-purpose credit cards, or paper-based proprietary or universal fleet cards at their retail locations. The major oil companies didn't think they needed us, at least not yet. In fact, they felt they brought far more value to this potential relationship than we did, especially once they realized that we had no customers to bring to their sites if they went through the work of integrating our specification. I heard many times, during the first three to five years when I was pitching our card to oil companies, "You've got to be kidding me!"

In one instance, I was told by a major oil company that they would never, ever accept our card, and all we had done was screw up the market. Fast-forward to a few years later, when the same company accepted our card. Talk about redemption. But it would take some time to get to that point.

THE COMPETITION

Next time you go to fuel your personal vehicle, look for the decals on the pump of the various cards accepted. You will see American Express, Visa, MasterCard, Discover, major debit network cards, the proprietary cards from oil companies along with WEX—and probably a few of our latecomer competitors.

But it wasn't always that way. In the 1980s and early '90s, it was only Amex, Visa, MasterCard, and Discover Card, which was launched in 1985–86 and slowly penetrated the market while facing the same chicken-or-egg conundrum on the consumer side that we faced with the oil company proprietary cards. They had millions of sites at which they needed to get the Discover card accepted before consumers would start to use the card for purchases. Our challenge was similar, but we needed 50,000 to 75,000 sites to accept our card before we could sign up fleets with thousands of vehicles. Even the major debit cards were not accepted until the early 1990s when the electronic point-of-sale deployment enabled a debit card PIN authorization.

And yet, WEX—this little fledgling company out of Maine—believed it belonged in the market and displayed on the pump. Convincing the oil companies to accommodate us, however, remained an uphill battle.

The oil companies posed a monumental challenge. This was largely why the VCs spent $23 million over eight years before WEX finally made a profit. During that time, we knew very well that no VC would continue to invest its capital unless we were able to demonstrate we could solve the card-acceptance challenge.

We needed a plan and we came up with one that proved—in time—to be a very good one. If you recall, as I mentioned earlier, the major oil companies made up 55 percent of the market. This meant that the midsize regional oil companies made up most of the remaining 45 percent of the market, and they most likely, did not have a proprietary card processing center of their own.

Our market intelligence highlighted that middle-tier oil companies would be our target market. This included companies like Getty with about 2,000 locations; American Petrofina, which was popular in the Southeast and the Southwest with roughly 3,000 locations; Circle K, running its convenience stores with about 3,000 fueling locations; and the French-owned Total, with roughly 2,500 stations in the Michigan, Indiana, Wisconsin, and the Rocky Mountain region, to name a few. Individually, none of these companies had 12,000 to 15,000 gas stations like Texaco, Mobil, or the major oil companies, but they did if we could string a number of these brands together. Individually, they were also not in thirty to forty states like the major players, but were generally found in roughly seven to ten states each. However, together they spanned the country.

Therefore, if we could get many of them to accept our card, we could give the WEX fleet card the national visibility we needed to sign larger fleets. Also, unlike Texaco or Mobil, they did not have the capabilities to develop a proprietary electronic-based fleet card in-house. They needed an outside third party to process either consumer or commercial cards for them for such an undertaking. By embracing our innovative product, they would get their own branded fleet card, plus they would enjoy a speed-to-market advantage that provided them with a head start when it came to penetrating this huge fleet market.

So, from 1986 through 1990, we strategically set our sights on this middle tier of oil marketers and were able to demonstrate the need and the value of the product we had built. We would support the operational aspects of managing their proprietary branded fleet card on their behalf, and it would be accepted only through their branded sites—effectively, a private-label product.

This also meant we would manage the contact center, the reporting, and billing to the fleets that were signed up to use their new electronic fleet card at their branded locations. Providing them their own proprietary fleet card gave them differentiation in the marketplace against the major players. In effect, they would have something that the majors did not yet have, giving them a leg up—which would become a huge selling point for us.

Unlike the original business model, this new model of back-end service fulfillment demonstrated a drastic departure from the franchisee model. We committed to doing this fulfillment even though it was at a time when we were still losing money. Under the franchise model, the oil marketers would fulfill all back-end services. This need to manage the back-end fulfillment services ourselves meant we were playing with fire: the VCs had to invest even more capital to enable us to build, staff, and manage this commitment.

From the perspective of the oil companies, it wasn't blind faith, but the oil companies had to trust us to deliver. They had to have faith that we would succeed both as a going concern and to manage their new fleet customers with quality services. This level of increased investment and fulfillment created an even greater risk. Our reputation was on the line. I became fully aware of the negative consequences, even personally, to my reputation and career if I ever wanted to reenter the oil industry, assuming we failed to deliver on our many commitments. But I knew we were on the right track, with the right business model. My job now was to convince the petroleum companies to trust us, to trust me, and to buy into our vision and our capabilities.

My petroleum background helped me establish a rapport and credibility with the oil executives. They could tell I understood their business and how WEX could integrate into their retail environment with little disruption. I spoke their language. And while I was taking on a massive responsibility, a risk that posed dire consequences for my career if unsuccessful, it was also my passion, my cause. It was something in which I had confidence that we could accomplish successfully.

THE BOLD WEX FLEET CARD VISION

Our vision was bolder than just offering the oil companies a proprietary private-label card that would differentiate them in this new electronic fleet-fueling market. We inherently knew that to optimize fleet penetration, especially large fleets, we needed the WEX card accepted at multiple brands across the country.

Actually, the easy part was to convince them to have us be their private-label partner, which simultaneously enhanced their brand. We made it mandatory for the oil companies that wanted us to process their proprietary fleet card to also agree to accept the WEX fleet card. Execution of this strategy would be critical for the future growth of the company. This most important strategic imperative was reinforced when, over time, we found that our most profitable fleet card program was the WEX fleet card. Today we have more cardholders on the WEX fleet card than we have on all private-label partner cards or on all co-branded card programs.

The hard part, however, was getting them to agree to also build into their point-of-sale electronic authorization terminals the acceptance of the WEX fleet card specification. We had to put forward a compelling and convincing rationale for them to also put our card specs into their devices. There was some resistance from the oil companies, asking us why they should accept the WEX fleet card in addition to their own proprietary fleet cards.

Our challenge was to convince them that the value proposition for them was that they would now be able to accept the fleets that we signed up. Since they didn't have a footprint in many other states, they couldn't accommodate all the fueling needs of large multi-regional or national fleets, but they could get those fleets to potentially use their branded sites in their region by accepting the WEX card.

In the states in which they did have locations, this would open up more fleet business to them by being part of the WEX card acceptance network. It was imperative for us to convince and assure our newfound partners that this would eventually be beneficial to them. We would be able to sign fleets that required a footprint beyond their proprietary retail sites and they would reap the benefits.

Part of what we were doing with respect to the private-label card and the WEX card acceptance model was similar to what TV cable companies had to do to accomplish their goals. Until they laid enough of the cable out there and until they could hook up the users on the other end, they were not going to have any business or make any money. They also had to make a big initial investment to lay all that cable. We were essentially "laying our cable" through the oil companies, but they, not WEX, were determining how fast that cable would be rolled out. The success of rolling out more acceptance of our card products was critical to cracking the chicken-or-egg quandary.

WORKING BOTH SIDES OF THE BUSINESS

By 1990, we had eight midsize petroleum marketers marketing their proprietary fleet card. Their combined retail locations totaled about 15,000 that also accepted the WEX Fleet Card. Our plan was working and fleets were signing up, but the acceptance of the large fleets was still too slow because we only had 10 percent of the US fueling locations accepting the WEX fleet card, which didn't satisfy a large fleet's convenience of fuel site need for their drivers.

But we were able to validate pieces of our business model by working with the midsize oil marketers to essentially solve the chicken-or-egg dilemma: we were getting card acceptance at their branded sites, and we were able to get smaller fleets to sign on to primarily use their proprietary fleet product. We were on a tireless mission to get more fleets on one hand and more oil companies on the other. The benefits to each side were proving that the business model was working.

So, we proved one important validation. Fleets would use this innovative fleet card product as long as there were convenient locations for them along their routes. However, the harsh reality was, we were still losing money. The fleet market penetration opportunities were limited to smaller vehicle fleets by deploying primarily a private-label petroleum marketer fleet card that was only accepted at their branded sites. The other problem was that the oil companies moved very slowly. It took time to get the oils to say "Yes"; then it took even more time to implement and download our specification at their sites. Only with sufficient site acceptance could our WEX fleet sales force go out and sell larger fleets on the premise that we had more oil companies on board. Back and forth we went, more locations meant more fleets and more fleets meant more locations. Initially, it was a slow process, but there was no other way.

We had to bide our time and be patient, hoping the VCs didn't run out of patience and we didn't run out of money.

To truly be successful, we needed to unleash the power of the WEX card, but that would require broad-based petroleum company acceptance, which still meant getting the major oil companies, at some point, to agree to accept our WEX Fleet Card and they were the ones still responding with a snarky, "You've got to be kidding me."

Our trials and tribulations to solve the chicken-or-egg conundrum and establish the WEX card acceptance were reflected in a few key developments of this second startup phase.

Once Parker left WEX, we experienced a little bit of a revolving door, with four presidents struggling to establish consistency and, in some cases, convince the VCs not to worry, that they could lead WEX successfully. Prior to the third president coming on board, we also had a period when we were without a president. This was a time when a few of us on the management team, together with a few VCs, comprised the office of the president "by committee" and ran the company. This is one of the benefits of having a team that stays in place for several years and goes through infancy together, which most of us had done during the first and second infancy periods. We were able to work together, stepping into this somewhat awkward position and keeping everything afloat.

During this period, we were essentially running on life support. To make matters worse, the VCs were concerned about the painfully slow growth; they felt that a reasonable financial return was in question. At that time, they were not wrong in their thinking. During the summer of 1990, we had exhausted our current VC funding and ran out of money to pay our bills and cover payroll. Consequently, our mainframe computer supplier, used by many credit card processors and network providers that move credit card transactions, had not been paid. Subsequently, they came to our data center and repossessed their computer. Things did not look promising. Our luck had run out, or so it seemed.

It's a bit of a crazy story as to how this played out. It shows how close we were to going out of business. All we knew was the computer supplier came in on a Friday to repossess the computer, knocked a big hole in the doorway (yes, computers were quite large at that time), and rolled the computer out. It was really devastating for the people at WEX because they saw firsthand what was happening. They could now read the writing on the wall... *literally, as transactions that were our life blood were dropping on the floor with no mainframe to catch and process them.*

At the time, I was in New Hampshire on vacation. I had just called in to the office to see how things were going, and somebody said, "Uh-oh, the computer company was in today, pulled the computer, and I think it's over." I made a few phone calls and rushed back to the office to say goodbye to all my people; I thought it really was over. All I could think was, "I uprooted my family and we moved to Portland, Maine—and now I have to start looking for a new job. And my reputation in the oil industry will be negatively impacted."

We had concluded it was lights out for WEX. A few days later, we found out that there was an ad for the computer in the computer company's newsletter. It was easy to discern whom it belonged to based on its type and its current location, plus the fact that there weren't many companies in Portland doing credit card transactions.

Then, suddenly, we were thrown a life raft at the eleventh hour. A few days after the computer was removed, Bill Richardson, our board chairman, a member of the founding family, and Parker's uncle, wrote a check for approximately $500,000 to pay the computer company and to assure our payroll until such a time when we could hopefully secure additional VC funding. By some miracle, we survived even though we were convinced, at the time, our doors would be permanently closed. Much to my surprise, and thanks to "Uncle Bill," the story of WEX was far from over.

In the relatively small oil company industry, word of this latest development spread fast and inadvertently alarmed the petroleum marketers being serviced by WEX. The eight marketers who had entrusted their brand to us in the fleet-fueling card business heard the news as it passed through the grapevine; one of the eight was told our computer had been repossessed over that fateful weekend. Because of the repossession, they all decided to hold a clandestine meeting and did not invite WEX or even disclose the meeting to us.

By the time they met, they probably knew we had gotten the computer back. But think about it: if you were running an oil company, and your supplier of services almost went out of business, it would only be natural to think, "Wait a second. What's going on here?" They were clearly coming together to protect their interests in this new program they all had rolled out with WEX. Circle K, Getty, FINA, Total, Sheetz, Quik Trip, Mapco, and Crown, at that time, inevitably had a lot on the line.

We discovered all this after the fact, of course. In the meeting, the eight oil company leaders or representatives went around the table—agreeing to never talk about terms or pricing—just sharing what they had been told by WEX, primarily by me, about our current status and circumstances. We were told later on that a number of questions were tossed around including, do we believe this company is going to survive? Do we believe that Mike Dubyak and the company have been straight and honest with us? Can we at least feel good about that? They knew we weren't making money—we were very clear about that—but they wanted to make sure they weren't being deceived in any way.

It may not have been all rosy, but there was definitely a silver lining in this cloud: all eight marketers mutually agreed that WEX and I had been completely honest in what I had conveyed to them regarding our status. Despite some of the bleak details, they took comfort in the fact that we were upfront and consistent in our messaging.

Once we heard about this covert meeting, we immediately invited all eight companies to Portland for our initial Private-Label Partner Meeting to discuss future plans and product enhancements. We wanted the opportunity this time to be in the room with them face-to-face. (We have hosted such a partner meeting ever since, and in subsequent years the company has, happily, been in a much healthier place.)

Though the circumstances were not ideal, that clandestine meeting, unexpectedly, established an even greater level of trust with each of these companies. Within the petroleum industry, it's a small group of key players, and people do communicate with each other. The long-term consequence was that our integrity and brand were actually enhanced, not damaged.

CULTURAL IMPACTS

I remember all of this intimately, almost as though it was yesterday. To this day, I honor and respect what each of these mid-tier oil companies meant to our fundamental success. They were our pioneers. They stood by us, helped us crack the chicken-or-egg dilemma and validated our value proposition, helping us move toward profitability and toward establishing greater value in the WEX brand.

We owe it to them for taking a chance on us, a small company in Portland, Maine with a big vision and an unrelenting drive. Our success with them validated our business model and was the reason the major oil companies eventually realized the value of our program and agreed to accept the WEX fleet card.

Through this process, it became apparent that there are various important aspects to a successful business plan, and the initial franchise business model missed the mark on understanding the financial dynamics of the petroleum industry profit margins. This lack of understanding meant that these initially targeted independent marketers would not invest aggressively to roll out sufficient sites with WEX to satisfy the fleet sales levels we needed to be successful. If we had stayed mired in the old way of doing business, the franchise strategy, we would not have been able to move WEX toward a profitable business model in a reasonable period of time, if at all.

This lesson would serve as a basis for future endeavors that WEX would entertain and sometimes pursue in expanding its business model. Also, knowing how we pivoted to 2.0 was not only an example of realizing the flaws in the first business plan, but also salvaging those positive attributes of the product to develop a revised business plan that put forward a new, more plausible, vision for success. I played an instrumental role in developing and selling this new concept and model. And in our case, the revised model would eventually achieve a much bolder result.

Even then, the road had many blind spots that required our team to navigate the unexpected without losing momentum or focus. Such was the case for WEX cracking the chicken-or-the-egg predicament.

We were confident the market would adopt our product, but we had to develop a strategy that enabled us to optimize solicitation of fleets while the window of opportunity existed, and before competition diluted our efforts and our first-mover advantage. Furthermore, we understood that the one critical cultural value in a strategic business to business model (B2B) is trust, which was a hallmark of WEX. Even in the face of adversity, WEX never compromised this value, which helped elevate our brand and ultimately propel and sustain our success in signing and partnering with multiple competing partners. It was and still is a fundamental "brick" in our cultural make-up.

The parental stewardship created a scenario that did seem like a "burning platform," in that we couldn't just ride on hope alone. It would have been foolhardy to proceed with the attitude that "all would work out over time." We knew time was of the essence, a factor not in our favor—we needed to either get off the burning platform or put out the fire.

In addition, we developed a competency in segmenting and marketing this innovative product to a very large fleet market. All of this was critical to our early success and has been enhanced over time. This rich and powerful history helped define who we are as a business entity. It has become inherent in our values and competencies, consistently differentiating us in the market. We'll talk more about the value of knowing, and teaching new employees, about our company history in the next chapter.

Meanwhile, we had cracked the chicken-or-egg dilemma, and now, great new opportunities with some inherent surprises were about to hatch.

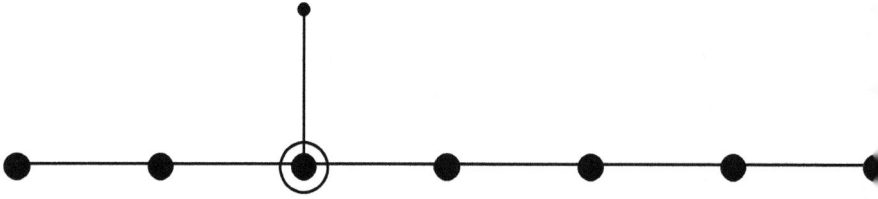

EARLY CHILDHOOD (1990–1993)

Chapter 4
The Tipping Point and Unexpected Competitor

The early phases of a new business may have some critical breakthroughs, but also many major developmental surprises, much like that of a young child.

In this stage of development, the child is standing, walking, and hopefully, getting ready to run. Likewise, a business model starts to achieve some financial stability and sustenance, but it still needs to prove that it has the ability to balance, accelerate, and maybe even sprint when the time is right.

PARENTAL GUIDANCE

At this point, the Wright family had exited the business and my understanding was that they essentially got their investment back, but decided that they could not, or would not, continue to participate in future funding rounds. The VCs were now in complete control and sensing the new business model was finding some level of success. However, they were starting to question how long and how expensive it would be to realize a reasonably favorable return.

Remember, VCs are not as a rule known for their patience, and they had been extremely patient with us for over five years as we now entered 1990. The private-label fleet card model had limitations standing in the way of it achieving explosive growth, and that was a red flag to the VCs. Consequently, we churned through some VCs who discontinued funding us since we were still losing money. This churning also meant that management pretty regularly had to travel to prospective VCs to convey the business model and try to convince them to agree to participate in the funding of WEX. It diverted our attention but was necessary for obvious reasons.

In addition, WEX saw president number four exit during this stage, and subsequently, president number five was introduced. However, president number four would make a surprising reentry into the market in a few years. The president's seat became a bit of a revolving door because either the VCs were unrealistic in their expectations of some or the presidents were simply too optimistic on the growth realities. Notwithstanding, we were fortunate to have a strong senior management team below the president who continued to drive the business as the presidential turnstile kept revolving. The core senior management team was convinced that we had finally found the pathway to success and we were committed and passionate about driving the business.

The VCs realized the value and capabilities of the core senior team, and even though we were churning through presidents, they basically kept the rest of the core senior team in place, which we were thankful for, even though at times we were surprised and amazed, because we definitely thought a major senior team management change was in the works. This was the story at many VC-run companies, yet it did not happen to us, and we gave the VCs credit and high marks for not targeting our core senior team. It was the president's seat that was the hot one up to this time.

PHYSICAL BEING: ENTER TEXACO

The tipping point, as defined by Malcolm Gladwell in his 2002 bestselling book *The Tipping Point: How Little Things Can Make a Big Difference*, is "that magic moment when an idea, trend, or social behavior crosses a threshold, tips, and spreads like wildfire." I had spent my career working in the oil industry and I understood the ins and outs, how parts of it worked, and how the key players responded to trends. I knew I just needed *one major oil company to say yes* to crack the code, solve the chicken-or-egg dilemma once and for all and to finally experience the tipping point—and it was about to happen.

Our tipping point, and ultimately defining moment, arrived in 1990, with the signing of Texaco. Up until then, we were working with individual midsize oil companies, still pushing tirelessly to attract the major oils, but to no avail. The signing of Texaco was a critical point for us. However, nothing about this deal was simple. It had many complicated twists and turns. Yet when we finally put all the pieces together, it became a major milestone in the history of WEX. Unfortunately, in time the relationship developed into a competitive threat.

When we began our communication with Texaco, we were informed that they were building a new credit card center that would manage the electronic requirements of a new Texaco consumer card and would consume all their programming capacity. They knew the programming of their electronic fleet card would be in the queue, but they decided they wouldn't program both cards simultaneously. They elected to focus on the consumer card, as likely 80 to 90 percent of their proprietary card business was on that card.

In the United States, there are approximately 250 million motor vehicles and about forty million of those are commercial vehicles; thus, there are a lot more consumers than there are commercial fleets, so it was understandable that they would put their primary focus on their consumer card conversion. Texaco was now convinced that an electronic proprietary fleet card was an important product entry to convert their paper-based fleets, as it was crucial for them not to be late to the game. They needed to avoid the possibility of their customer base eroding now that new electronic fleet card options were becoming available in the market through their competitors.

WEX was creating market impact, and it was causing some level of urgency for Texaco to consider in hopes of not missing the window of opportunity when it came to introducing an electronic fleet card. Ultimately, Texaco negotiated with us to process their proprietary fleet card for two years, with the understanding that they would then take it back in-house once they were ready to program and operate their proprietary fleet card on their new system. This was fine by us, knowing we would now be processing for one of the largest oil companies in the country, and this would further elevate our brand and business model.

Another big selling point for them, although it was not explicitly mentioned but was mutually understood, was that they would probably go to school on us because they were going to eventually program their own proprietary card. By working closely with us, and seeing our product in action, they would learn the ins and the outs of best practices and product functionality, which they could then program into their own fleet card. What we didn't know or realize was that this learning experience would eventually become a broader competitive threat.

When it came to them accepting the WEX universal fleet card, I made it clear in our negotiations that we would not cave in on our requirement to have them also accept the WEX card. This was part of our arrangement with all the midsize oil companies, and we were determined to hold to our principles with Texaco. Initially they said no. Then they tried another route, wanting an exclusive as the only major oil company to accept the WEX card. This was also something we could not agree to, so it prolonged the negotiations. Some of our selling points to Texaco included trying to convince them that by becoming the first major oil company to accept the WEX card, we believed they would realize a big advantage over any major oil company that came six months, a year later, or two years later and agreed to accept the WEX fleet card. The WEX card fleet drivers would develop a routine of going into Texaco's stations and using our card. Furthermore, in Florida, Texaco had recently acquired some retail fueling locations that were already accepting the WEX fleet card and were enjoying a strong level of WEX card sales. We made it clear that Texaco would lose this WEX card volume if they didn't accept the WEX card at all their 15,000 sites.

On top of all of this, WEX was feeling added pressure from the VCs because there was always that lingering doubt as to whether or not they were really going to sign. In the end, we prevailed. Now, their 15,000 locations were added to our existing 15,000 WEX card accepting sites and we could start to go after larger fleets with this new footprint of 30,000 retail fueling sites.

As a result of our new relationship with Texaco, two things happened. First, the larger fleets with hundreds of vehicles started signing up to use the WEX card and second, the acceptance momentum would now begin as the major oil companies, that I was consistently meeting with, began to change their tune. They were all very competitive with Texaco and with each other, so they just could not let Texaco reap the rewards of being the only major oil that would enjoy the fleet sales volume on the WEX card. So, one by one, from the early to late 1990s, all the major oils agreed to accept the WEX card. Many times within the oil industry, if one major company moves in a certain direction, others are going to follow suit if they see it's a worthwhile path. Once we secured Texaco, the other major oils started questioning, and asking, "Why is Texaco doing this? If Texaco is doing this and realizing a benefit, shouldn't we also be doing this?"

Even the major oil company that said, "We will never ever accept your card," conceded. By the way, they held out and were a late adopter, but when they eventually conceded, they called me up and surprised me by saying over the phone, "We give!" You could not have scripted it any better than that for sweet redemption. What drove them to concede was that they realized that many of the Bell Company's fleet drivers, who used to stop at their stations to buy fuel, were no longer stopping there to buy fuel and merchandise because they did not accept the WEX card. At this point, if they wanted to compete for the large fleets they had to concede and accept the WEX fleet card.

The tipping point for us on the fleet side was the signing of Bell South around late 1993 with 18,000 vehicles in nine southeastern states including the Carolinas, Florida, Georgia, and Tennessee. They signed and exclusively had their drivers only go to stations that accepted the WEX card. We would then use them as a lighthouse account and could now go after other Bell companies and large regional, and national, fleets. The Bell Company fleet managers communicated with each other, and the people at Bell South told other Bell companies that our program delivered great product functionality, which delivered the promised security and control value proposition. We eventually signed other Bell companies like Ameritech, which also had nearly 18,000 vehicles in Ohio, Illinois, Indiana, Michigan, and Wisconsin and Southwestern Bell, which covers Texas, Oklahoma, Arkansas, and other states with some 22,000 vehicles. Just as Texaco meant more fleets would sign, the major Bell fleets and other large fleets meant more big oil companies would agree to accept the WEX Fleet Card. We were solving the chicken-or-egg dilemma by growing significantly on each side of the equation.

It was our bold vision, along with grit, and steadfastly holding to our principles that made this happen. If we had compromised on any of these principles that were key to our long-term, bold strategy, our future potential to optimize market penetration and our level of success might have been limited. Sure, we might have had a profitable business only processing proprietary cards for oil companies, but we would never have reached the level of success we enjoyed by having our own WEX fleet card introduced in the market.

Backtracking a little: getting Texaco on board was the breakthrough moment that really helped us eventually get the WEX card accepted deeper into the market. I can still remember it like it was yesterday—getting the long-awaited fax in my office signed by Texaco—and what a celebration we had, knowing that we finally got it signed, and we now had a major oil company accepting the WEX card.

PHYSICALITY: THE TEXACO TWIST

As planned, somewhere around the end of 1992 or early in 1993, Texaco brought their proprietary fleet card in-house for processing at their new card processing center. However, when a company decides to build a processing center, as Texaco did, they have to be competitive with alternative processing options to make such an endeavor worthwhile and able to contend. Conversely, at the same time Texaco was building this new card processing center, there was a movement by the other major oil companies to start outsourcing their credit card programs to third party processors that could lower the oil company's cost because of the scale they created by managing multiple consumer and commercial card programs across multiple industries, not just oil company cards.

So, the BPs, CITGOs, Exxons, Chevrons, and Mobils of the world started to say, "I'm going to outsource and close my processing centers down because there are companies that can do this cheaper than we can do it on our own. There are companies that can fund our receivables when we should be putting our capital to work seeking out more oil resources, building better refineries, and enhancing our stations." However, Texaco, which had taken the opposite route, by building a new processing center, now appeared to be searching for ways to bring more business into their processing center to lower their cost, while attempting to be competitive with the third-party processors. This apparent need to process more transactions at their new processing center ultimately changed the course of our relationship with them.

Up to this time, we believed we had a mutually beneficial relationship. We had provided them with a quicker head start in the electronic fleet card market, and they were enjoying increasingly ramping sales at their retail sites by accepting the WEX fleet card. What we didn't know or expect was that something much bigger was taking place behind the scenes. They did more than learn from us as they designed the processing of the Texaco fleet card. In the early 1990s, shortly after Texaco brought their proprietary fleet card in-house for processing, they requested a meeting, flew up to Maine, and asked us one very puzzling question: "Would you like to have all your fleet cards processed by us on our new card platform? We could become your third-party processor." We were taken aback. Why would we want to process our fleet cards through their processing center and lose direct control of development and processing for ourselves? And why would we want to do this on behalf of the other oil companies for which we were already doing the processing? After all, we were in the fleet card processing business. So, we said, "No thank you." We wanted direct control over programming new functionality and management of our transaction processing. We wanted to maintain our own proprietary control and not give control over to a third party. They understood that.

While we turned down their request to become our processor, we later found out that they would eventually solicit many, if not all, of the independent oil companies we had signed up to process their private-label fleet cards. Many of our private-label oil company partners, we were told, were approached by Texaco and asked if they could compete and process these WEX partner fleet cards! Effectively, they were competing directly with us as a third-party fleet card processor, and trying to go after the very same independent oil companies that had put our startup company from Portland, Maine on the map.

Fortunately, and to our benefit, these midsize oil companies gave a standard reply of "No, thank you," across the board. We believe they did so for a couple of reasons. First, it seemed apparent to us that they didn't want a competing oil company having all their fleet customers' data residing on Texaco's database and feared the possibility of Texaco potentially targeting their business. After all, Texaco was first and foremost a competing oil company, not primarily in the business of processing proprietary cards, so this offer could not have sounded very plausible to these mid-tier companies. But more significantly, we believed that we had built and nurtured these relationships over several years and had demonstrated that, along with an innovative product and great service, they received our loyalty, honesty, and integrity—three attributes that were integral to WEX. These independent oil companies trusted us and respected the product value we offered them. They were not going to walk away from WEX and sign with, of all parties, another oil company. Needless to say, we appreciated their loyalty.

As we tried to understand what was driving Texaco's behavior, we believed that they were internally trying to justify to their senior management team why their decision to build a new processing center was a good one. We concluded that by soliciting, and hopefully, signing either WEX or other companies and becoming a third-party processor themselves, they were trying to lower their transaction cost in their new processing center. By doing so they could better compete with the cost of these third-party outsourcing providers and not find themselves in an uncompetitive position.

What we also didn't know or expect was something much bigger that was taking place behind the scenes once the third-party processing strategy failed to establish any new processing business for them. Essentially, it appeared to us, once some of these other strategies didn't materialize, they pursued an alternative strategy to bring in more transactions in their new card center. And they did just that in a move that involved creating a direct competing product to the WEX fleet card that changed the course of our relationship with them.

In the mid-1990s, Texaco called me down to Houston, Texas, where they dropped a bombshell. In this meeting, they revealed to me that they were creating a product called Voyager, a universal fleet card that we would come to learn was positioned to compete directly with our universal fleet card, the WEX card. The real revelation was not that they were going to accept the card only at their branded locations, but that they had been soliciting all the other major oil companies to accept their card, the same ones we signed to accept our WEX fleet card. They had been soliciting them with a pitch that focused on winning over California's state fleet card business, which was substantial. Their selling proposition to the other major oil companies was this: "We'd like you to accept this card. We're going to have it accepted at your locations and our locations, and you'll get your appropriate share of the state's fleet business!" Their rationale was that to win a state's fleet card business you needed to be able to bill the state fleet net of specific taxes and, at the time, the WEX fleet card was not able to do that. Texaco's tax group was geared to manage such a process, since they were already doing tax exemption on their proprietary Texaco fleet card.

During this meeting, Texaco tried very hard to play it down and assured us that, in fact, they *wouldn't* be a direct competitor of ours. They positioned it that they were primarily doing this with the other major oil companies to win California's fleet card business, looking particularly for the government fleets that benefitted from a tax-exempt status when purchasing fuel. It was more of a shock, just listening to them justify and rationalize this by explaining how they were going to start using the Voyager card in a very specific piece of the fleet marketplace but somehow, they didn't feel that area of the marketplace was going to be in competition with WEX since we did not yet have the tax-exempt status built into our cards—yet we certainly would make that available in the future. So, I inquired if instead of launching Voyager they would be willing to offer the tax-exempt billing process to WEX so we could compete for the California state fleet card business on the WEX fleet card. This request was not acceptable to Texaco.

We knew that if they were successful in securing this piece of business that they were going after, they would also go after other parts of the large fleet market we were now growing in, areas that did not require tax exemption. And that's exactly what happened. What they were really saying was, "We're coming into the market and we're going to be a competitor." They started by targeting the same oil companies and we knew that eventually, they would start going after the same fleets that we were either serving or soliciting. The facts spoke for themselves.

All I was thinking about during this meeting was, "Wow, they not only went to school on us, but they basically created, and were now introducing, a competing product that would pose a major threat to the WEX fleet card."

Although I never imagined this would happen, I did have an inkling of what was going to be revealed before a few of us boarded our flight to Houston for the meeting. However, I was just hoping it wasn't going to play out like this. We were warned by a few of the major oil companies that had been solicited by Texaco. They called us and basically said, "Hey, we're being approached by Texaco to accept a new universal fleet card product in California. Do you know anything about it?"

At the time, WEX didn't have all the facts, nor did we know how much truth was behind this, but when we got called down to Texas, we pretty much knew that was what they were going to unveil to us. So it wasn't like we were completely blindsided. Nonetheless, it was a shock to hear that they were actually talking to the same oil companies that we had signed to accept the WEX fleet card and soliciting them to accept their new Voyager card.

Ironically, it also turned out that one of the former WEX presidents, who found himself in the president's hot seat during the venture capital stage, was hired by Texaco and became the first president of the Voyager card. Texaco already had the inside scoop on our processing capabilities. Now the hiring of our former president provided greater insight into some of our strategies, which they could use to better compete with WEX with the Voyager card.

To be honest, it was quite a disappointment to find out that Texaco turned the tables on us and were now going to compete with us. We went from the discussions back in 1990, when we were going to help them process their proprietary card, to giving them a first-mover advantage on the WEX card, where they were already reaping the benefits, to finding out that they had morphed into a universal card competitor to the WEX card. That was a bitter pill to swallow. I remember celebrating the day we signed them as our first major oil company and how much that meant to all of us. I also remember the sense of betrayal when we found out that they were to become our competitor. It was almost like the joy of a wedding and the later disappointment of a divorce.

Yet as disappointing as this scenario was, we were convinced they had reasons for choosing to introduce a universal card. If you analyze the developments, which began with them wanting to process the fleet cards for WEX, as well as for other oil companies, and now creating the Voyager card, it reinforced our speculation that since they had built this new credit center, they needed to justify that it was competitive. They had to increase processing throughout to lower their transaction costs and to maintain, or even validate, the expense of creating and running the center, as compared to outsourcing the processing.

As it would turn out, Texaco was eventually bought, and their new owner eventually outsourced all card processing, which would include the Texaco portfolios. So, in effect, they would no longer process their own fleet cards. As for the Voyager card, it is still a competitor to WEX today, although a smaller competitor. The Voyager card portfolio was eventually sold a few times, and today it's owned by U.S. Bank, which is a leading provider of commercial card products.

Even though this happened back in the 1990s, there is a lesson to be learned: be consistent in your strategy and how you build long lasting partnerships. But don't assume that all partnerships are built on the same principles, such as creating mutual benefit. There may be other circumstances, which you may be unaware of, that could change a partnership into a competitive situation. Therefore, whenever possible, be careful who your partners are and what intentions, or agendas, they might be harboring.

In the bigger picture, the silver lining is that the whole trend for the major oil companies to outsource would eventually prove advantageous for us. Over time it meant that we'd have the opportunity to win and to process the private-label cards for other major oil brands. Today, WEX has over twenty oil companies that it does the private-label processing for, so that whole trend of outsourcing really worked to the advantage of WEX.

CULTURAL IMPLICATIONS

Because of my longevity with the company, I understood the founding family's importance to our birth and funding, and its belief in our future, even after we pivoted and reconstituted the business model. I recognize how important the midsize oil companies were to our early success; they were the strategic solution to cracking the chicken-or-egg dilemma for us and validating our business model. I also appreciated the fleet owners who recognized the value proposition we offered and with whom we formed trusting relationships.

I strongly believe our integrity helped us forge strong bonds with these strategic partners in a B2B business model, where we knew a win-win partnership had to be developed and sustained. I know how important these early partnerships were in fulfilling our bold vision of having the WEX card eventually accepted at over 90 percent of the 150,000 or so retail fueling sites. In addition, I also recognize how critical it was for WEX to hold to our principle of not compromising the requirement for a private-label oil partner to also accept the WEX card. Furthermore, over time, I felt it was important for the new employees to not only understand how the signing of Texaco was a major milestone and tipping point in our road to success, but also to understanding how a competitor, Voyager, was eventually created by Texaco. These themes became part of my communication strategy to all new WEX associates.

Up until the time I stepped down as CEO, I hosted a New Employee Orientation (NEO) luncheon where I would present our new employees with a snapshot of our rich history. This was something that was very important to me, to show where we had come from and the challenges we had overcome—and how this had a huge influence both on our growing success in the marketplace and in helping to shape the foundation of our company's culture.

When I spoke at these luncheons I would begin by explaining why we were located in Portland, Maine the significance of the founding family in the greater Portland area, and most importantly, how they supported us through some tenuous times. I would convey how the private labels played such a critically important role in the pathway to success for WEX, when many factors posed huge challenges to our success.

By the end of one of our NEO luncheons, new employees would have a strong handle on how the WEX card found its way into the market and propelled our success. It was because this Maine-based fleet card company held firm to its strategy to have all private-label oil companies also accept the WEX card. Now they could identify with our strong values and principles, which helped formulate our cultural attributes and pathways to success. Most importantly, I hoped the new associates were able to realize that our company's values were based on integrity and grounded in treating our partners and fleets with respect. I was also hopeful that the associates could better understand why

WEX worked hard to partner well with its employees and the communities we live in.

All of this was a big part of formulating a fundamental foundation of being a strong, respected, and trusted partner. So it was important to me that new employees who joined WEX would not look around and see a successful company with sophisticated processes and benefits and basically ask, "So, what's next?" I wanted them to identify with the struggles we overcame, and how these challenges helped forge our foundational character. Our foundation of character included innovation, boldness, persistence, grit, vision, trust, integrity, and respect for the founding family, investors, and early adopters.

Associates had to buy into this cultural underpinning, and yet, I explained how in the early years our associates had not yet become a focal point. For instance, they didn't receive competitive medical benefits for many years, nor were there any formal training programs or even career development processes. This wasn't because these benefits were not important, but because when you're losing money and trying to prove you can become a going concern, certain aspects of the business will be compromised for a while, but only for that while.

This was our history, and yet, these employees in the NEO luncheon knew how much we were investing in our people, with benefits that included healthy living, training, and development, maximum matching on their 401K, and recognition programs that not only incentivized, but also focused on how employees could grow their careers within WEX.

I wanted all associates to be proud of what WEX represents, feel invested, energized, and ready to be a part of its future success and bold vision.

In an era of tremendous turnover in businesses, it is now as important as ever to not only offer benefits and "reasons to stay," but also to build a foundation from which people should want to believe in a business model. Today, there are companies that are growing and retaining employees not just because they are profitable, but largely because of how they conduct themselves. If they demonstrate respect for their customers and their associates, people are attracted to the care and benevolence demonstrated.

This is important because it's easy to attract people when everything is going well, but it is also easy to lose them when the market and/or the business reverses its course. You want people who believe in the company's culture as strongly as we did, and who will still be there to roll up their sleeves and work hard during the tough times rather than bailing out.

Believe me, there were plenty of times when most of us on the management team at WEX could have given plenty of good reasons for bailing, but we didn't and consequently, today's management feels great pride that we stayed the course. It's important that new employees know that the company has seen its ups and downs and that not everything in the company's history was rosy. Tell your company story and don't sugarcoat it. Your employees will benefit from hearing the true story and better appreciate how the history shaped the culture and business model.

MIDDLE TO LATE CHILDHOOD
(1993–1996)

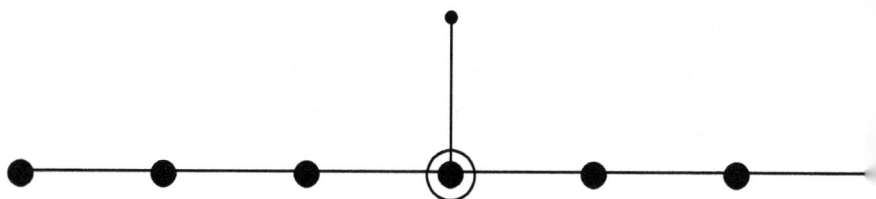

Chapter 5
Cultivating a Winning Culture for a Competitive Edge

---

*When you begin to grow strong, you believe you are invincible,
but sometimes parents lack confidence and you are forced to grow
up fast and be independent in spite of them.*

Middle to late childhood is a time when all the physical attributes of the business are defined and the business is beginning to pick up momentum. A great deal of energy and resources were now being placed on the external aspects of the business with increased site acceptance and developing the go-to-market channels, while little attention was given to the internal workings of the organization and the human resources. In spite of this imbalance and the outward focus, the business model had been validated and the opportunity to optimize market penetration was in full force. It was during the end of this period that the business ingenuity started to serve as a source of creative inspiration, more than ever.

PARENTAL GUIDANCE—TIRED OR ANGRY

By 1993, the VCs had invested $23 million, which, in those days, was a substantial amount of VC money. They were starting to see a return on their investment. In 1993, we had our first profitable year, where we were able to generate over $300,000 in profits; and in 1994, we were on track to attain approximately $1 million of profit. This was an exciting time at WEX, as we were now on the road to making money and having sustainability.

An important event took place when the board added our first non-VC board member in 1993, a credit card industry expert, who was tapped shortly after joining our board to run Safecard Services, Inc. in Jacksonville, Florida. He had great insight into WEX's business model, and one of his first moves in his new role as CEO of Safecard was to make an offer to buy Wright Express for $34 million.

At this time, some VCs were tired and convinced by both the then-president (number five) and the chairman that although we were going to see our sales grow, we were not going to grow aggressively, and we would not realize the potential of the proverbial hockey-stick growth. In addition, it was my understanding that a case was made, by these two corporate executives, that we should be worried that MasterCard, Visa, or Amex would potentially enter our fleet card market and have a material impact on our growth prospects. Other VCs, however, were bullish about the future and did not believe that the sales would be leveling off or that the competitive forces were imminent or a significant threat.

The worst aspect of this entire scenario was that I had put together a three-year forecast projecting future sales and revenues and presented those figures to the president before I left for a vacation in Europe. This forecast was intended to help the president and the VCs make their decision about whether or not to sell WEX. My forecast was based on trends and was realistic yet, over time, proved to be conservative. During my discussion with the president I asked him to hold off on any presentation to the VCs, and any subsequent vote, until I returned from Europe. I believed it was important for me to be in front of the board presenting the forecast in person. Unfortunately, I never had the opportunity to make that presentation.

To my dismay, while I was out of the country, I was told that the president downward-adjusted my projections to reflect a slower ramping of sales and revenues, and the newly edited forecast was presented to the VCs, illustrating a much smaller growth rate than the one I had submitted. The president had his concerns about the competition and, as I understand it, tried to make the case that companies like MasterCard, Visa, or American Express could easily duplicate what we had put in place, and that our growth would be compromised by such a competitive threat in the near future. Of course, all of this was based on speculation, since nobody had any real information that indicated these credit card giants had plans to move into the fleet card market.

It was my understanding also that the president was pushing hard trying to convince the VCs to vote for selling the company. The board went forward with a vote determining whether to hold or sell the company. The share vote was approximately 55 percent to 45 percent in favor of making a sale. As a result, the more optimistic, bullish VCs were angry about making this premature exit.

Even more disappointing was that management never had a chance to try to formulate a management buyout (MBO) since our president was apparently in favor of the sale and pushing hard for it. What I discovered when I returned from my trip was that our current president had apparently orchestrated a soft landing for himself as the new president and COO of our new parent, Safecard. He would no longer be president of WEX but, in his new role, he would be reporting to the industry expert who had been on our board, now the CEO and chairman of Safecard.

This was not a good development for most of the WEX management team. We had worked very hard to make WEX a success and wanted to see our stock options eventually provide a reasonable payoff. We had been convinced that we were now on track to increase the value of WEX and make that happen. Needless to say, many of us were very disappointed. It was now 1994, so I'd been at WEX for eight years. In fact, it was not uncommon to find members of the senior management team who had been at WEX seven to nine years. What we received for our efforts, once our stock option value was monetized, was disappointing. You can imagine that this was a bitter pill to swallow. We had believed that we were finally on the right track for high, or even explosive, growth.

If somebody had said to me—and I think this goes for many of the senior management team other than the CEO— "Would all of you like to buy this company? Could you go out and raise private equity or venture capital money, whatever funds were needed to buy the company?" I think we would have put our hands up and said, "Absolutely! Let's go try to get this done." We never had the opportunity because the full senior management team wasn't on board with this possibility and unbeknownst to us talks were happening behind the scenes and deals were being made behind closed doors.

Naturally, on many fronts, this was a big disappointment in that we, as senior management, were not getting the opportunity to entertain, or try to put together, a management buyout as an alternative option. This was frustrating because most of us believed our future prospects for success were amazingly bright. Over time, we were proven right, but the result of WEX being sold was, as we were about to find out, just the beginning of a wild ride with constantly changing parents.

PARENTAL GUIDANCE—SAFECARD 1994–1996 AND CUC 1996

Safecard was a credit card insurance company. They were a silent partner that offered credit card insurance to many of the major credit card–issuing companies, such as banks, and across multiple industries. This meant that customers would pay a monthly fee on their credit card and if they lost or had a credit card stolen and reported it, they would have no financial exposure. The credit card company would then mail them a new card within days. This business model offered a great benefit for consumers, but it was not really applicable or synergistic to WEX and our fleet card program.

It had been rumored that the former WEX board member who became CEO and Chairman of Safecard apparently lost the confidence of his board of directors when he failed to successfully diversify Safecard after making significant investments in new ventures that apparently didn't provide reasonable returns, as far as the board was concerned. In fact, another board member soon replaced him as CEO. The board of Safecard then agreed to sell the company, including WEX, to CUC International in 1996.

The bottom line was, when it came to ownership of WEX, Safecard really left us alone. We ran the business as usual, since Safecard had few synergistic opportunities for WEX to take advantage of and they added little value to our business model. We were swept up in a quick exit orchestrated by their board.

At WEX, we were now onto president number six, who was hired by Safecard and ran WEX under Safecard and now the new parent company CUC. We had a new parent and a new CEO, and we just kept our heads down and continued concentrating on our rapidly expanding opportunities. We soon found out that the new CEO, who appreciated that we were on the cusp of explosive growth, would eventually pursue a management buyout when the opportunity presented itself. When these new developments eventually unfolded later in 1998, it caused great excitement to think we might finally get our independence.

PHYSICALITY—GO-TO-MARKET DIVERSIFICATION

Based on the establishment of the private-label oil company card products, and the emergence of the WEX fleet card, we had now established two ways to access or market the fleets: first through the oil companies' proprietary private-label fleet card product, and then with the WEX universal fleet card. As we were starting to see the major oil companies agreeing to accept the WEX universal card, we also started signing large fleets to use the WEX Fleet Card exclusively.

In the last chapter, we discussed how some of the "baby" Bells, like Bell South, Ameritech, and SBC had signed on to use the WEX card. It was during this period of time, 1993–1996, that we were not only able to bring such major regional fleets on board but were also able to sign national fleets.

This further accelerated the signing up of the oil companies to accept the WEX card so they could realize their fair share of the large fleets' business at their retail locations. Clearly the momentum of one side of the equation was propelling the other. The more fleets we signed, the more oil company acceptance we were able to realize.

Concurrently, more oil company acceptance led to signing of larger regional and national fleets. Now we could also utilize these major fleets that were using the WEX card as "lighthouse" accounts to help promote and convince other fleets to consider signing and realizing the benefits of our electronic fleet card program. Likewise, fleets that were using the card made it easier to sell the idea of card acceptance to the oil companies, knowing that they did not want to be left out when it came to gaining business from these many WEX fleet customers. Suddenly, there was no more chicken-or-egg dilemma because instead of trying to get one side or the other (fleets or oils) to move forward, both sides were essentially prompting the other to sign up.

We had worked so hard for this development and now to see it materializing was not just validating, but it was also energizing as we began to think bolder and bigger in our expectations and overall vision. We had oil companies that were initially adamant to not accept the card, saying "I give." There were also others that thought they controlled parts of the country with their market share and had initially rejected us, who were now, slowly, conceding to accept the WEX card.

With this bolder WEX emerging, another development materialized that led to the establishment of our third major go-to-market strategy. In the early 1990s we approached GE Fleet Leasing to provide WEX with access to their National Account Program. Keep in mind the fleet leasing arm of GE was wrapped under GE Capital. The GE National Account Program was accepted at over 40,000 major vehicle service providers, including Firestone, Goodyear, Jiffy Lube, Safelite Auto Glass, and many more major service brands. The strategy we jointly developed enabled us to market this acceptance to our WEX fleets and the private-label oil company fleets. Now we had the ability to expand functionality on the card beyond fuel to include all vehicle-related operating needs and services. Just the reality of this offer enhanced the stature of WEX in the market. We worked for the better part of a year to get ready to effectively launch this new product diversification. We updated fleet marketing materials and prepared our sales organization to unveil this new fleet service opportunity.

WEX was very successful in the marketing of the service, but we soon realized that the combined program was a hybrid of an electronic card acceptance at fuel locations with a paper-based service acceptance through the GE network of service providers. Apparently, we did such a great job of convincing the fleets that the electronic acceptance of the fleet card at fuel sites provided them with security, control, and savings, that when they realized that the GE service program was paper-based, and did not provide the same level of security and control, they were disappointed.

As a result, sales, which started strong, quickly tailed off. GE and WEX both understood and accepted the dynamics of why the program never took off. As it would turn out, WEX would eventually try putting an electronic service provider program in place in the mid-1990s on its own. We tried to replicate the oil company electronic paradigm, but soon realized the service provider electronic acceptance situation was very different and much more complex. The rollout of an effective electronic service provider program would take many, many years to realize. Today, WEX can claim the acceptance of the service cards at over 40,000 service provider sites, which includes electronic and some level of paper acceptance, depending on the service provider.

Getting back to GE, we were able to demonstrate to them that we were a capable company and partner. The fleet growth on the WEX card was ramping up and the oil companies were starting to agree to accept the WEX Fleet Card. Keep in mind that GE was the largest fleet leasing company in the United States at the time, with over 400,000 vehicles leased to corporations for their fleet vehicle needs.

Up until that time, GE supplied their fleets with a paper-based universal fleet card accepted at virtually every oil company brand. When we approached them we wanted them to consider doing a co-branded WEX/GE card that would access the sites accepting the WEX card, and we would pass the electronic information on to them so they could bill their fleet customers for the fuel purchased on the co-branded card.

This product offered efficient and streamlined information, which was superior in every way to their paper-based fleet card. The GE name would be prominently placed on the face of the card for their fleets to identify with their leasing partner, GE, but the card also had the WEX logo on it so the oil companies knew it was a WEX card and would accept it for payment.

This meant that if they accepted the WEX card, they would accept this card as another flavor of the WEX Fleet Card business. Eventually, we were successful in signing GE to be our first co-branded partner and we would work closely with their sales force to help convert their fleets to the new co-branded card. The only shortcoming of the WEX card versus their paper-based universal fleet card was that acceptance at oil branded sites was still greater on the GE paper-based card. Together we felt we could work together to overcome this deficiency.

However, we ran into another interesting situation when a major fleet provider of services, with a huge portfolio of fleets, wanted exclusivity in the fleet leasing market. We had a principle to be neutral as a partner to GE and other future potential leasing and co-branded partners. Nonetheless, we met with them and once again were across the table from a major company, explaining why we were not willing to accept an exclusive relationship.

Once again, we had to stand firm on our principle to not grant exclusivity to any partner. As you can imagine, this was not an easy discussion with a very large, and successful, industry-leading company in their respective market, but one with which we had to be firm and not compromise our future growth opportunities. Once they agreed to become a nonexclusive partner, we knew that with their influence we could once again speed up oil company adoption of the WEX Fleet Card.

As we continued to grow, GE saw the benefits to their fleets, and one of the GE representatives even accompanied me to meetings with a few major oil companies. He was able to express GE's desire to have the oil company accept the WEX card, and in that way, GE could accelerate the rollout of the co-branded card to their thousands of fleet customers who represented 400,000 vehicles. This was more leverage created by a very large company with a huge portfolio of fleets ready to utilize our new and innovative fleet card product.

Over time, we were able to sign six of the top fleet leasing companies to a co-branded product similar to that of GE. We could now attack the market with our direct channel, the WEX card, and through two distribution channels: private label and our newest channel, co-branded. Now more than ever, we had channels that would allow us to optimize penetration of this vast fleet market, either directly or through these powerful distribution channels.

During this evolving relationship with GE, we met with their private-label card group, which was also part of GE Capital. At the time, they were the largest provider of private-label partner cards to various types of retailers, including oil companies. They supplied both consumer and commercial private-label cards to their partners. Remember, oil companies had both consumer and fleet card customers and had begun outsourcing their card processing. GE was capable and ready to step into this new market opportunity.

Our hope was to convince them to consider WEX to become their fleet card partner in their private-label strategy, specifically for the major oil companies. Though the meeting was cordial, they were clear that they would be competing directly with us for the private-label fleet card business of the major oil companies and not partnering with WEX. Going into the meeting, we didn't believe this partnering opportunity would happen, but the meeting and request were still worth the inquiry.

We now had developed a strong relationship with the GE fleet leasing division, which greatly benefited our WEX Fleet Card strategy. However, when it came to the private-label oil business market, it became apparent that we would be competing with GE Card Services. It took a while, but over time we were successful in competing for major oil company private-label fleet card businesses against GE and other large third-party processors.

The market was now becoming more complex and we began to realize that we were both a utility for the private label and for the co-branded partners, respectively, and virtually a direct competitor to both channels by us selling the WEX card into the market. The competitive complexity involved oils not only competing with other oil companies who used our product, but also included competing with both WEX co-branded leasing partners and with the WEX universal card. Basically, a similar scenario existed for the co-branded partners who competed with other co-branded leasing partners, the private-label oils, and the WEX card.

Consequently, this channel-conflict situation required WEX to build a level of trust and integrity that would allow us to manage all these competitive forces and not lose the respective partner's business over time because of an apparent conflict of interest. We developed a set of principles regarding our rules of engagement that allowed all of us to compete for any and all fleet business, but where we would at least be crystal clear in how we would do this so that none of our partners would ever be caught off-guard or surprised by our actions in the market.

We had to convince our various partners that the ultimate arbitrator was the marketplace and any fleet would make their decision on how all of us bundled services to create value and win the fleets' business. In all cases, our commitment was to invest in world-class call centers and fulfillment services so the oil companies could be proud of how their customers were treated. Furthermore, we would continually invest in the products that would consistently differentiate our value in the market. They entrusted their brands to us to manage their fleet customers with the utmost care and valued products and services.

To this day, our strong commitment to provide exceptional fleet customer care has continued to differentiate us in the market. Essentially, we know we are in this for the long haul and want to create long-term partner relationships. We accomplish this by servicing the fleets on the WEX card or a partner card with a strong value proposition. I took a leadership role in consistently convincing and demonstrating that we could do this in a manner that would bring value to our partners. This helped cement our multiple and various partner relationships.

CULTURAL IMPLICATIONS

Now we were feeling the energy resulting from our success. We had unleashed the go-to-market ingenuity and creativity that we introduced into our business model that resulted in the creation of our co-branded line of business and further product enhancements. The WEX business model was in aggressive motion and we were adding both accepting oil companies and new fleet businesses, one propelling the adoption of the other.

Our direct sales channel was being ramped up rapidly, and our two distribution channels were expanding, and we were converting fleets to their cards. Now it was critically important to consider investing and planning for the future by putting in place a more balanced business model portfolio.

One big part of the balanced portfolio focus was our people. Vision, passion, and commitment helped us become a successful "going concern." We were energized by the bright future that lay ahead. More than ever, we had to truly respect the importance of our people and their significant role in sustaining our success.

We needed to encourage them in various ways to embrace and enhance our culture. We were creating intellectual capital by working on developing new product functionality, creating a world-class hybrid go-to-market distribution model, and committing to building world-class service centers.

We put together better and more comprehensive benefits for our employees and started to expand our human resource department to address the selection, development, and promotion of our people. In addition, we made it a priority and principle to promote from within whenever possible and consider external candidates only when it was absolutely necessary. People could enter WEX and quickly move into progressively more advanced positions and develop their careers. For example, there were two women who agreed to start at WEX as my executive assistants, but made it clear they had the background to move into more challenging roles over time. I'm happy to say that both fulfilled their career aspirations and both eventually assumed management roles at WEX. This situation repeated itself throughout WEX.

We also created recognition programs to celebrate the best and brightest people who were helping drive the success of business and who set the standard for others to emulate. Quarterly all-company meetings were implemented to provide insight into the various developments of the business, to give everyone some level of knowledge of what was going on and where we were going.

At these meetings, we instituted quarterly individual and team "WEXcellence" award winners. Then, once a year, we celebrated the annual WEX President's Club Winners, which was to honor those WEXers who demonstrated a body of work during the year that distinguished them in their department and in the company. The award announcement became an annual event that our employees looked forward to attending. The President's Club started with only a handful of winners and throughout the years has grown dramatically. As time went on and WEX grew its employee base, we had forty to fifty winners annually enjoying this most prestigious award.

The best aspect of the WEX President's Club, as well as the quarterly WEXcellence award winners program, is that they allow anyone in the company to nominate any employee at any level and in any department. We realized that if we wanted to show our deepest respect for every employee in the company, we had to open this distinguished achievement recognition program to everyone, not just have it heavily weighted toward the sales and marketing group, as many companies had done.

We also wanted to be fair across the board. We encouraged everyone to nominate any person whom they felt distinguished themselves in the company, regardless of their title or department. When selecting possible winners, we were looking to answer these questions: "In their role in the company, *what* did the nominee do that was special and really moved the company forward in some fashion?" Then we asked, "*How* did they do this in such a way that it validated and embraced the values important to making our culture part of our strategic advantage?"

The quarterly and annual awards have since become a WEX tradition. I strongly believe these awards have always sent an important message to our people, and that is: "We acknowledge that everyone is important to our success and *how* they behave is just as important as to *what* they achieved."

This type of recognition process is something we created and something I strongly believe in. As I mentioned earlier, my mother treated everybody equally and with respect and I always try to do the same in life and work. I believe in recognizing others on their own merits and for who they are as individuals. When someone goes above and beyond the call of duty to help make others' lives easier or achieve something great, you recognize them for their personal achievement and their effort.

You will also find that appreciating and recognizing the accomplishments of people at all levels of your business will help everyone buy into the mission of the company. People like to feel they belong to something larger than themselves. Whether it means taking an active role in their communities, volunteer organizations, sports or religious groups, there is a shared sense of participation that creates a sense of camaraderie and motivates people to try harder for the good of the group, organization, or business. They also want to be recognized for their contributions to this larger cause.

We developed a powerful group dynamic when we were working day and night to help WEX survive back in the early days, and I knew how powerful that feeling of being part of the process could be. When people feel that they are an integral part of the company, the team, or the business, they look forward to coming to work and have a sense of personal pride when the company succeeds.

I personally adhere to Dov Seidman's views in his 2007 book, *How: Why How We Do Anything Means Everything... in Business (and in Life)*, where he puts forward the concept that in our wired world the "what" is a must, a prerequisite to even being in business today, but the "how" is what will differentiate the winners.

Seidman's theme is one where you must not only outperform but also "out-behave" the competition to succeed in a significant way. Our philosophy at WEX aligned with that of

Seidman's in that it was important to recognize not only "what" was achieved, but "how" people accomplished their high level of achievement by modeling the company values.

We found that if you treat your employees as you treat your customers and partners, they will feel valued. Creating a positive experience for our trusted partners and customers was just as important to us. Just as we did with our employees, we nurtured these relationships by providing them with the best possible experience.

In a wired world, the communication options to talk about customer experience are readily available. Again, this is where we align with Seidman's views. He says if a company delivers on their commitments 99 out of 100 times, but their competition does it only 90 out of 100 times, the first company will win in the marketplace. We were actually practicing and embracing the Seidman view years before he wrote the book. I believe a company has the ability to fulfill its commitments consistently so that it becomes a driver of its sustainability and brand strength regardless of what the competition does.

Let's face it: brand is a lot about a customer's emotional investment in a product and company. The deeper the investment, the harder it is to displace the product or company. At WEX, we strive to make that emotional investment a positive and deep one for our partners and our fleets, as well as our associates. We have embraced this philosophy and, I would say, WEX recognized this cultural approach early on and formalized a recognition process to capture the essence and importance of both the power of the "what" and the "how" that has helped shape our culture and brand.

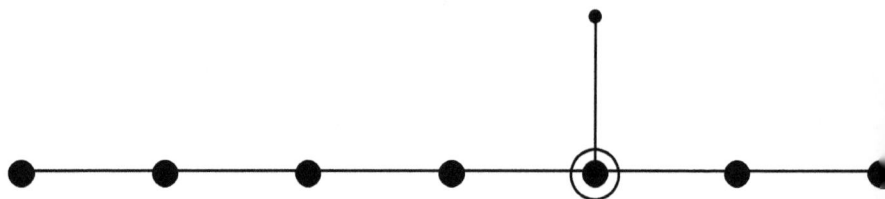

ADOLESCENCE
(1996–2001)

Chapter 6
Leadership: Baptism by Fire

Without regard to consequences, the young life of a business will enter the "constant experimental phase" also known as "the perpetual mode of immortality." Most important—an influential leader to direct this phase into its young adult life.

Despite the possibility of another sale looming over our heads, many of us remained passionate about the future of a company to which we had given so much of ourselves. We shared the realization that the business had great opportunities physically, emotionally, and culturally to define its future pathways for success. Physically the business was strong and able to take on more, but to sustain itself, more than ever, it would need to: (1) invest and build bench strength, (2) strive for a balanced portfolio, (3) balance short-term success with long-term success via strategic planning, (4)consider diversification of markets and products, (5) solidify the cultural attributes to sustain its success well into the future, and (6) manage its capital to achieve these various sustainable attributes and assets.

PARENTAL GUIDANCE: CUC INTERNATIONAL (1996–1998)

CUC provided consumer-based card enhancement services, like dining discounts, for cardholders of a particular brand. The core Safecard product fit very well with CUC's array of consumer card products, but for WEX there were no significant synergies, since we were serving businesses. The good news was that CUC's senior management acknowledged this fact and worked with the senior management of WEX to determine an enterprise value for the company so it could be purchased. This would allow them to come up with a price to sell the business to WEX management.

This was exciting news and it electrified the senior management team. Our business was in high gear and the future looked extremely bright. The President and COO of CUC met with senior management and communicated that we would eventually have the ability to finalize a management buyout and that the terms and value were basically negotiated. The caveat was that, since they had purchased Safecard with CUC stock, they were prohibited (by the SEC) from selling any of the Safecard assets for eighteen to twenty-four months, and WEX was one such asset that had to be held for this period.

While we needed to temper our enthusiasm, as we waited for the impending sale, a sense of excitement remained among the senior management team as we looked toward our future and eventual independence. And then, suddenly, the rug was pulled out from under us once again. We woke up one day, came to the office, and were told that CUC decided to merge with HFS to form a new company, Cendant.

Two critical developments led to what was a huge disappointment for the senior management team. First, it was discovered that CUC was inappropriately recording revenues to pump up their profits and keep their stock price on a constant upswing. Once discovered by the HFS management, post-merger, they had to report this circumstance, which resulted in the new company, Cendant, losing approximately half of its market cap in one day, and SEC investigations quickly ensued. The CUC management team was ousted and some eventually went to jail for their actions. (Note: WEX was not party to any accounting irregularities.) The severely wounded Cendant was now managed by the HFS team.

The second development was that we had no champion within Cendant to fulfill the eventual sale of WEX to its management, as promised by CUC. A Cendant management team, which was essentially HFS management, traveled to our headquarters in the summer of 1998 to deliver the devastating message in person. They made it crystal clear that they were glad they had taken ownership of WEX through the merger with CUC and liked what we had developed as a business model. They also made it clear that they had no intention of selling WEX to its management. Since the WEX management team was very focused on the eventual management buyout, this was yet another huge letdown.

Things moved fast following this jolting news, but not in a good way. You might say things began to unravel. This latest wrinkle in the WEX story resulted in the CEO of WEX leaving and me, as EVP, ultimately being promoted to CEO and president of WEX under Cendant. Had the circumstances been different, I would have celebrated this promotion, having given so much of my life to the company.

However, this was like being asked to serve as captain of a demoralized team. Needless to say, this was a difficult time for me. I was as devastated and disappointed as everyone else about the lost ownership opportunity and sincerely thought of leaving WEX. How many times can you be punched in the gut? But after careful contemplation and thoughtful introspection, I could not escape the fact that my commitment to WEX and to the state of Maine was still very strong. As a result, I agreed to take the reins. WEX remained my cause and I personally had a lot invested in its success up to this point. So, in August of 1998, I became president and CEO of WEX. Clearly, the fate of the company was, more than ever, in my hands and control.

PARENTAL GUIDANCE: CENDANT (1998–1999)

Here I was, CEO/president of WEX, hoping for a clean start, but tension and trauma would soon fill the air. After working to make a smooth transition from the previous CEO to my new leadership position, I was hoping to maximize future stability at the company. However, the exit of the CEO was a clear message to the management team that independence, at this time, had been lost and was no longer in the cards for WEX. But that was only one development within the company that made my baptism as president rocky and extremely challenging.

Just after I took the reins, we received the results of our first-ever employee survey, which devastated me. At the time, our employee turnover was greater than 40 percent. The survey basically conveyed the tough message that over 40 percent of our people were looking to leave the company within a year and that many in the company and especially in the tech services department expressed that WEX was a "churn and burn" environment.

Up to the time of the survey, I was heading up Sales and Marketing and we were delivering the goods and building great strength in the market. The Sales and Marketing teams were engaged, driven, and satisfied, seeing our impact in the market. It was especially disheartening to me to realize that outside of my corner of the world, so many people were so dissatisfied. Prior to that time, the rest of the company was not under my direct management responsibility, which included employee satisfaction. Now, I would make it a personal goal to turn this employee satisfaction level around, but I knew it would take time.

Making this considerable cultural turnaround even more difficult was that over the next few months, other senior people would also pack their bags and exit. They were either disappointed in the failure to complete a management buyout, chose to work for the former CEO who had started a new company (where he could promise independence), or they simply decided to pursue their own career paths outside of WEX. Some of these were long-time associates who had been through all the stages and WEX transitions with me. In fact, within the next year, five senior people would leave the company including our CFO and CIO. This was a very difficult time for me personally, to see friends and strong leaders exit the company. WEX was hurting and it was up to me stop the bleeding, so to speak.

Despite the mass exodus, I still believed in the company and would have to work hard with the HR team and the remaining management team to put new practices in place and renew the faith and belief that, at the core, we had a good product and we would thrive and survive. If I didn't sincerely believe this, I too might have left.

So, there I was, in charge during what was becoming one of the most challenging periods on the WEX timeline. It was a time of upheaval, disenchantment, high associate attrition at all levels, and major implementations to execute. It was baptism by fire, to put it mildly. But I got up every day and attacked the challenges to keep moving us forward. At times, I had as many as sixteen meetings in a day. I would start meeting with people, sometimes at seven in the morning, and have meetings virtually every half hour, or every hour, all the way until maybe six at night. Just meeting after meeting after meeting and it was exhausting, but there were too many fires burning that needed to be put out and the meetings were important to keep us moving forward.

The new Cendant brought yet another challenge. Our previous parents had no synergies with our B2B model, but HFS, now Cendant, owned PHH, a commercial vehicle leasing company that was using its own fleet card product to provide to their fleets. They were a competitor to one of our strongest distribution channels of our cards, the co-branded fleet leasing program. At first, we didn't see this as a problem since the PHH fleet card product was inferior to the co-branded card product used by our other fleet leasing companies. But our leasing partners were watching intently to see what would transpire over time. They were concerned that we might show favoritism to PHH when creating a fleet card relationship with PHH. They also had to be wondering, as we were, how WEX and PHH were going to coexist in the same company. Would there be some level of integration between the two companies? It was quite unusual to have one of the top leasing companies in the United States that was actually a fleet card competitor, under the same umbrella.

We could see that having both of us under the same roof, competing in the fleet card market was not a sustainable situation on many levels. So, we thought we should examine some ways in which we could work closer together. As it turned out, the team at PHH was also coming up with their own ideas, and as it would happen, they beat us to the punch with an idea about how working closer together wasn't in their plans. Theirs was a plan that we never saw coming.

Short of owning WEX ourselves, we thought an opportunity existed with this synergistic sister company that would provide a positive impact for WEX by embracing our products and retiring their proprietary fleet card. We were so wrong. In 1998, MasterCard developed a competing product to the WEX fleet card product. Of particular note is that one of the key architects of the MasterCard fleet card was a former WEX executive who left WEX prior to us being sold in 1994. Just as in the case of Voyager, the product capabilities and key leaders for the competition had ties back to WEX. Their card was initially developed primarily to compete for the federal government's fleet business, which was, at that time, in the range of 900,000 vehicles. PHH decided to embrace this new MasterCard fleet card for use in their market to compete directly against WEX and the co-branded partners we had signed on.

But as we were to find out, this was only the tip of the iceberg. Then came the big surprise, as I was invited by PHH to a meeting at MasterCard headquarters to discuss "potential synergistic opportunities." Approaching the meeting, I was not aware that WEX was "THE Opportunity."

I remember sitting there, with a few people from PHH and the head of card marketing for MasterCard and the former WEX executive mentioned above, when it became apparent to me from the conversation, that PHH had pledged a quantity of roughly a million fleet cards that would be converted to the MasterCard fleet card program. This would allow PHH to receive a substantial discount on pricing from MasterCard. I quickly realized that the only way to get to the number of cards pledged by PHH was by including some of the WEX card portfolio. PHH had maybe 250,000 cards deployed, certainly not millions. The only one at this table who had millions of fleet cards was WEX, and I was sitting there representing WEX, fully aware that I never pledged our million plus cards to anyone. As a matter of fact, there had been no prior discussions with the PHH management on this topic.

At that point in the meeting, I literally called a timeout and even made the sports timeout signal, putting one hand over the other making a T and saying "timeout." Realizing what was going on, I leaned in and said to everyone's full attention, "Wait a second, I was not a party to this commitment by PHH and did not agree to it." I explained that I was not committing our WEX cards to a MasterCard fleet card or to anyone else and that as far as I was concerned, this meeting was over. And with that, I headed to the door, ending the meeting abruptly. I remember thinking, as I headed back to my office, about how PHH was essentially trying to pull the rug out, not only from me, but from the people of WEX. We had developed our own product that ran on our own systems. Were we now supposed to just give all of that up because of a commitment someone made independently without even including us in their plans?

Consequently, I decided that I should meet with my boss at Cendant, who also had PHH reporting to him. I wanted to see if he also shared my enthusiasm for all that we had accomplished and would continue to accomplish with our products at WEX. Luckily, he was willing to listen to our strategic plans and how the WEX product, price structure, and go-to-market plans would prevail in the marketplace. He even came to Portland, sat down with me and my team, in the conference room, and we had a full-day presentation. At the end of the day he said, "Just keep doing what you're doing; I'm not going to disrupt anything." That was great. He gave WEX a chance to prove our strategies and we demonstrated great growth and market leadership, which he and Cendant continued to completely support.

Then in 1999, Cendant decided to run an auction to sell WEX and PHH together to another company. The ultimate winner of the auction was Avis. Keep in mind that Avis was 20 percent–owned by Cendant and because of that ownership position, Cendant had Avis board seats. Some people speculated that this sale to Avis was going to happen, but they needed to test the value in the market. Regardless, we were now in a newly formed company that was all vehicle related. This was the first

Chapter Six: Leadership: Baptism by Fire

time that we were part of any organization where we felt like the parent had a related interest and potential synergies.

PARENTAL GUIDANCE: AVIS (1999–2001)

Under Avis, we were even closer together to our competitor, PHH, and our leasing partners were watching intently to see what would come of this relationship. Needless to say, they were skeptical and concerned that we would offer PHH preferential treatment. What they didn't know was that "preferential treatment" was not at all what I wanted to offer PHH.

When the dust settled on the new Avis, there was good news for WEX. Clearly, the CEO/President of Avis understood the components and the strengths of what he had acquired. He made it clear, organizationally and strategically, that the Avis part of the business was the rental arm of this new company, PHH was the fleet leasing entity, and WEX was the card provider. By demonstrating once more our capabilities, competency, expertise, and value, we found a way to survive and thrive in this new entity.

How do you spell relief? "AVIS!" This now meant that we were no longer directly competing in the fleet card arena with PHH but we would be supplying PHH with our card products. Now I had to meet with the other fleet leasing companies to assure them that we would keep PHH at arm's length in regard to contractual and pricing terms. I met some of these leasing company representatives, the CEOs, face-to-face, while some

121

wanted our reassurance in writing, and others just took my word for it. My commitment to each of them was that, over time, it would become clear that we would never put PHH in a position to have any advantage over them. We would have an arm's length relationship with them when it came to pricing or creating strategic value.

We demonstrated and lived up to this commitment, and our trust and integrity as a partner was further ingrained and enhanced. The irony regarding PHH was, of course, that they were a competitor who at one point wanted to team with MasterCard to take control of our fleet card business, and in turn, we ended up running the entire fleet card business for Avis, which include PHH. I might note another irony which took place back in the early 1990s. PHH came to meet with WEX about a possible acquisition. After meeting with us, they then decided not to make the purchase because they believed they could do better on their own and didn't see us adding value to their plans. With regard to the fleet card business, it appears WEX prevailed again.

However, it also became clear to us that part of the strategy for Cendant to sell PHH and WEX to Avis was to drive up the Avis stock price, which would have been beneficial for Cendant as 20 percent owners in Avis. Unfortunately, this stock lift did not materialize as was envisioned. If this had happened, Cendant would have realized the positive impact on the stock they owned in Avis, which would have created a strong return for them.

In the end, the failure of the stock appreciation strategy eventually resulted in Cendant deciding to make an offer to purchase all of Avis, including WEX and PHH, and, once again, we were one of at least fifteen Cendant-owned companies.

PHYSICALITY: FLEET PAYMENTS

Be careful what you wish for. Around 1998 we were able to negotiate the fleet card conversion of a US major oil company and, separately, its Canadian sister company. In both cases, we would be converting hundreds of thousands of fleet cardholders onto our systems. Securing these partnerships was a huge win for WEX and for me, knowing I was EVP when we signed these two strategic companies. We would also be required to program in the fleet card features that were unique to the oil companies' product and different from the WEX core product set.

Up to that point, we had only used the WEX spec for all oil company private-label programs and had never taken on the programming task of building another fleet card spec into our systems. The plan was to convert the portfolios on to the WEX system by late 1998. The reality, which soon became clear, was that we wouldn't be able to do the conversion until early 1999, at the earliest. I was the EVP of Sales and Marketing when we signed these large partners but was promoted to president/CEO in August of 1998, about the time that the conversions were to happen.

Keep in mind that this was the period in 1998 when Cendant informed us we would not be able to complete the management buyout, my predecessor left the company, others were getting ready to exit, the employee survey uncovered a high level of dissatisfaction, and our tech services organization was facing difficult challenges with these large conversions and keeping up with our accelerating growth.

One of the executives that decided to leave WEX at the end of 1998 and join the former WEX CEO was our CIO, which meant we had to recruit and bring in a new CIO in the middle of converting these very large portfolios to the WEX processing system. To make matters worse, on top of all these challenging forces, the oil company fleet card conversions did not go well; actually, they went very poorly. This was truly the most difficult and frightening time I had ever experienced in the market at WEX. The conversions were rife with errors and problems. We had to fix problems on the fly, and the fixes would take the better part of 1999 to implement.

During this tumultuous conversion process in the summer of 1999, two of the major oil company representatives, who had championed converting their business to WEX and with whom I had built a great relationship, sat down with me for a meeting on the status of the conversions. They informed me during the meeting that if they had to do it over again, they would not have supported the signing and conversion to WEX. Knowing how hard I had worked to make WEX the premier supplier of fleet card services in the United States and how their signing with WEX helped reinforce this position, their message crushed me. They had researched us for a few years before signing with us and surmised that we were innovators, a progressive company in the fleet card market. They believed in our capabilities and signed with us to be their fleet card processor. It was a major step for us because we were not going to provide them our product but instead would be converting their product onto our system. Unfortunately, we essentially dropped the ball. Not only did the conversion process take longer than anticipated, but when we issued invoices and reports to the fleets we began getting phone calls about errors. We had major problems and, to make a long story short, it took quite some time to clean up the mess.

I was especially distressed through this time period, because for years I had championed WEX and took pride in the company and our achievements, and here we had the opportunity to take on a major piece of business and elevate our stature and brand to a new heightened level. The reality that they were disappointed was devastating professionally and personally. I vowed to work through this situation and over time restore trust with this important partner. I also knew this was a long-term challenge and not a quick fix. The oil reps heard me, but surely had their doubts as they left the meeting.

We worked tirelessly and diligently to win back the trust of the major oil companies by consistently demonstrating follow-through on commitments made to them and to our partnership after the initial program implementation. It took years, but in time we were able to obtain this renewed trust in our overall service capabilities. I think this was best demonstrated when it was time for them to renew their contract with us and they not only renewed the contract, but signed on for a long-term contract. In addition, we later had the opportunity to expand with them internationally in a meaningful way and we have continued to demonstrate the ability to meet or exceed their expectations of supplying world-class products and services. I still feel vindicated that we were able to turn around the initial disappointment to where today, WEX enjoys a very strategic, healthy, and expanded relationship with this critical and key partner.

It shows that if you make an error in business, rather than trying to run from it, hide from it, or pass on the blame, you need to own up and do everything in your power to fix it… and then go the extra mile if possible. That's what we did and now, years later, we can take pride in our ability to have rectified the situation, regained our credibility, plus signed a long-term agreement.

PHYSICALITY: VIRTUAL CARD

In 2000, when the CEO of Avis declared they were the rental car provider, PHH the leasing provider, and WEX the card provider of the new Avis, it also meant that we would inherit the MasterCard fleet card, as well as the travel and entertainment (T&E) card relationships from PHH. Yes, the same MasterCard that was targeted to supplant the WEX card products.

Since WEX had a specialty bank in Salt Lake City, we had the legal structure and ability to issue a MasterCard commercial card product directly. There are a few benefits to having a specialty bank, known initially as an industrial loan corporation bank, or ILC, today an industrial bank. Most significantly the federal government had grandfathered Utah to have specialty banks. These banks do not have branches and are not able to take deposits from consumers, but most importantly, they do have the ability to export Utah usury law to all fifty states. In effect, bypassing the usury laws in each state made the specialty bank an efficient way to uniformly extend credit across the United States. Over time there have been companies like BMW, Harley Davidson, Target, American Express, and WEX using these banks because they need to grant credit across the United States. We all have a preference not to manage the compliance of the various state usury laws, but because of the Utah bank charter we only had to comply with Utah law. This saves countless hours and money spent on lawyers in each state having to keep up with fifty sets of different usury laws.

Our goal was to convert all the PHH cards to a co-branded WEX fleet card product, which left a small portfolio of MasterCard T&E cards. By taking over and issuing the T&E cards, through our bank, we provided a diversification opportunity for WEX, beyond fleet cards, where we could potentially develop a new product opportunity and possibly bring value to an emerging new market. Easier said than done, but we had been innovative before.

Many of the big banks that issued commercial Visa and/or MasterCard solutions, along with Amex's commercial card products, were providing commercial cards to businesses of all sizes for their typical travel and entertainment purchases and for typical purchasing card requirements. The reality for WEX is that we could not reasonably compete head-to-head in such a crowded and saturated space dominated by very large players who had scale. Our goal was to find a way to provide deep product capability in an attractive niche market, possibly a relatively new or unique market opportunity. With that in mind, we had such an opportunity present itself after a meeting with Priceline in 2000. They were a pioneer in online travel account (OTA) services and were just emerging with their new online strategy to change the way consumers secured their travel needs. They were not yet profitable but were carving out a new market with the unique idea of allowing consumers to book travel online and shop for the most competitive rates for hotels, airlines, and car rentals all in one place on their online site.

What we discovered was that their management systems and processes for paying hotels had become somewhat cumbersome, inefficient, inaccurate, and difficult for them to manage. They had built an in-house solution to pay the merchants, but they knew that as they grew it would not provide a viable solution. By listening carefully to Priceline's challenges, we had an opportunity to step in with a solution whereby we could provide security and control (a similar value proposition to our fleet card) in a specific segment of their market.

There are approximately 40,000 hotels in the United States alone, most of which are franchises that want to receive their money quickly for any hotel bookings through Priceline. (Note: In the universe of rental car and airline companies there are dozens of providers, not 40,000, to manage through online travel services. Consequently, the reconciliation process for Priceline directly was easier and more manageable for online rental car and airline payments.) Priceline had to meet the consumer demand when someone was booking online, but at the hotel end of the transaction there were some major, and costly, problems in terms of back-office reconciliation. It might have been a case of mismatched online booking dollars received by Priceline up front from the consumer when they locked in their price of the room versus actual consumer hotel purchases that were put through by the hotels. The difference in dollar amounts came from the extras that people charged to the room, such as the mini bar, room service, dining in hotel restaurants, and other room charges.

Even at that early stage, Priceline had over forty people assigned to manage this back-office reconciliation. To remedy the situation, WEX devised a single-use ghost account (SUGA, today called a virtual card transaction) for every online booking that was sent off to the hotel once the consumer booking was locked in. When the consumer came to the hotel to fulfill their stay and checked out, the hotel would have this unique MasterCard SUGA account number that would only authorize the dollar amount booked by the consumer initially online. It would not honor any ancillary charges spent at the hotel. No physical card was present to fulfill the transaction, which is why we now call such a transaction a virtual card transaction. By separating the booking of the actual room onto the ghost account from the additional expenses to be paid by the customer to the hotel, we made life much easier for Priceline.

Ultimately, we were able to decrease the forty-some people in the back office who were managing Priceline's reconciliation process down to just a few people. It was an elegant solution to an unruly process that was critical for Priceline to become successful with their online hotel process, especially realizing the size of their program today.

In this particular market, we have been successful by providing our virtual card product to many of the largest online travel companies in the United States and around the globe. This was, and still is, our primary product and market for the virtual card segment of WEX. We have found other markets for the virtual card, but so far, just not as large as the online travel market. Even this new market and product diversification was on shaky financial footing for the first five years.

We did not turn a profit in this diversification strategy until 2005, and every year we would thoroughly examine the product's financial viability. We had to answer these questions: did we meet our goals and expectations for the year and was the market opportunity still attractive? Should we continue to invest in this product and market? There were some years where we were close to the point of pulling the plug, but we assessed progress against plans, quantitatively and qualitatively, and in hindsight, made the correct decision every year to persevere. Today, greater than 20 percent of the revenues come from the virtual payments segment of WEX. Once again, we provided a very specific product solution for partners that enhanced their overall value proposition.

CULTURE

This period became a turning point for WEX. We would now go to work to embrace our commitment to be an employer of choice, not one where we were a temporary stopping point for someone looking to further his or her career. Also, more than ever we would work to repair the loss of confidence created by the rocky implementation with two major oil partners.

In an effort to constantly improve our employee satisfaction, we continued to poll our employees roughly every eighteen months or so to understand their satisfaction levels. Every survey resulted in our entire management team working to understand and address the key themes of dissatisfaction.

Managers would then methodically put together specific action plans for them personally. They would then be asked to implement and later be judged, in their yearly performance evaluations, on how well they did implementing the plan.

I am happy to report that in my last eight or so years we had employee satisfaction levels that were considered world class, except for one year, where we barely missed the world-class distinction. Our employee turnover rate was down to 10 to 15 percent in virtually every one of those years (versus the 40 percent level in 1998). We were able to realize that our culture had become a strategic advantage, helping to drive strong customer and partner loyalty and satisfaction. Because of this world-class associate satisfaction, we found that our people became more engaged and committed to our success. The company continued to enjoy industry-leading customer satisfaction levels born out in high card activation rates and low card attrition rates. Today, the culture has become a strategic advantage in WEX's B2B business model, where partners experience a consistent win-win relationship.

With respect to the new endeavor into the virtual card market, we were able to deploy innovation in developing an elegant solution for the online travel market fulfillment predicament. It demonstrated another development of a product capability that was not yet available in the market. WEX took an innovative pioneering role in creating a new solution of precision that helped the partner save money and delivered a superior service for their customers. This product solution became a critical part of their overall value proposition. We were also able to draw on our struggles during our early years with the fleet card to better manage, nourish, and gauge the financial and resource commitment to this new product and market. Today, our virtual card program has solidified the cornerstone of the WEX diversification strategy.

Looking back at the illegal activities of CUC, the disappointment of not having a management buyout, the departure of so many key WEX team members, PHH trying to severely jeopardize our business model, and the conversion nightmare of 1998 and 1999, I realized that these were the most challenging years of my long career. In addition, family issues arose and I needed to step away from WEX for a few months during this time period to fly over to Europe to take care of my daughter and help my wife out while she was trying to help her family during a health crisis. I guess that's what the adolescent years are all about, numerous challenges that you need to take on or overcome to grow stronger. That's what those years were for WEX, and I guess you might say they were a second adolescence in a way for me personally, as I stepped into the president/CEO role, with a lot to learn and overcome. Looking back today, it was all worth it.

EARLY ADULTHOOD (2001–2005)

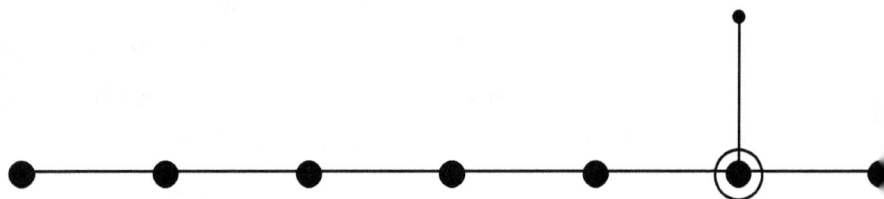

Chapter 7
The Final Road to Freedom...at Last

There comes a time in everyone's life where taking a chance, making a bold move is contemplated. However, not everyone decides to step out and take the chance, because the outcome may be too uncertain. But sometimes, past experiences make the bold move an easy decision.

Early adulthood is a time when one begins focusing more closely on building and securing their future. For WEX, this meant making our mark and perhaps even securing that long elusive road to independence. To forge ahead meant acting on the strengths developed with the company's early successes and fortifying the foundation for a long-lasting existence. It also meant the company should be innovative with our physical attributes to build on strategies that would allow us to succeed in a more mature state of competition. There was also a need to start searching for ways to diversify our capabilities in order to minimize the vulnerability of having only one core product.

PARENTAL GUIDANCE: CENDANT (2001–2005)

The good news was that PHH was converting all their cards, proprietary or MasterCard, to WEX co-branded fleet cards. It wasn't easy, but at the end of the day, we eliminated a competitor and reaped the benefit of their large card portfolio. Our other leasing partners stuck with us, and for the next few years, WEX continued to grow, but our marketplace was heating up. A few of our competitors found it too difficult to get their proprietary card accepted at all the oil companies, as we had done over the years. So many of them decided to ride the MasterCard oil company acceptance network and use a MasterCard fleet card product to compete with our broadly accepted network and product. As they say, success breeds competition, which was very much the case.

By 2004, the fleet card chessboard was in play and getting very competitive, more so than ever before. This meant we needed more latitude. Otherwise, when we looked into the future, we could see our business model being compromised and our value possibly being diminished. So, in the summer of 2004, Melissa Smith, our CFO at that time (later to become CEO as of January 1, 2014), and Rowland Moriarty joined me to meet with my Cendant boss, as well as some other Cendant executives, for a meeting in New York. Rowland (Row) had become a consultant at WEX back in 1994 and helped us develop our go-to-market strategies as well as our overall strategies. Over time, he became a friend of WEX and provided counsel to me on business developments of various sorts. He also became a trusted adviser and wanted to see WEX optimize its success on many dimensions and fronts.

My management team and I were always looking for ways to move the company forward without compromising our growth and success. At the New York meeting, we discussed the competitive developments occurring in our market and, because of the competitive marketplace, there existed the potential for Cendant to experience a compromised value over time with WEX if they did not allow us more latitude to play on the strategic chessboard in our core fleet card market, domestically or internationally.

We knew that we could end up on either side of a double-edged sword. Either Cendant would decide to sell us before they experienced a compromised value for the company, or they could allow us to invest in our business through acquisitions. Since Cendant had experienced merger and acquisition experts who bought and sold companies routinely, and since we were doing well and experiencing positive cash flow, there was a possibility that they could be supportive if we were in a position to make acquisitions. They knew if there was consolidation going on in our market, it would have been very easy for them to back us up by having us use their M&A group and by deploying our strong cash flow to help us buy some companies. Cendant was even supportive as we had the opportunity to meet with some companies about possibly acquiring them as part of this process.

The good news was that Cendant knew we were ready to be proactive and increase our value, rather than allowing inactivity on the chessboard to compromise our enterprise value. The message was delivered and apparently acknowledged. As I mentioned above, we initially pursued some opportunities, but they weren't going to materialize at this time. It then felt like we were entering a period of limbo, unsure of whether we would pursue being a buyer or be the ones being sold. The future was unclear and more than a little unsettling. But remember, we had been through six owners, so unsettling was familiar territory for us.

Ultimately, Cendant decided to jettison us, under the right conditions. The only question was how this would this happen. Having already had many past parents we were not anxious to find ourselves with someone new. Every time we were sold it created a challenging transition that would take a toll on the culture of the business, since our people would wonder if their jobs were in jeopardy or if any major shake-ups would transpire.

The timing of this news from Cendant, however, came at an opportune moment. It was the fall of 2004 and Google had recently gone public, which energized the Initial Public Offering (IPO) market. Several investment bankers convinced Cendant that they could maximize their extracted value for WEX through an IPO, if they could ride the very positive wave developed by the Google IPO. Finally, a path materialized where we could be sold to the public market and take control of our own destiny, at least we hoped.

We were quite aware that a positive IPO window could close at any time, if conditions caused the market to go sour and new public entrant valuations were to become depressed for any new market entries. If the newfound IPO market value optimization was lost, then WEX could be headed for another disappointment by landing with another new parent instead of enjoying our independence. In fact, even if the IPO market value remained strong, if another company was willing to top the potential IPO value, we could still be sold by Cendant. Therefore, we had to temper our enthusiasm about the possible IPO. We also had to act quickly.

AGGRESSIVE BEHAVIOR

Being strategic thinkers, we knew we needed to initiate the discussions and possible outcomes by taking matters into our own hands or at least do as much as possible, considering Cendant still held the proverbial cards. We knew we were not a core asset for Cendant and, therefore, doing nothing was not an option, so we could not risk sitting idly by and watching as our market consolidated and became more competitive. If we were standing on the sidelines as the battle intensified, we would observe our competitors getting stronger, which could weaken our position. Ultimately, we could find ourselves being purchased at some point while not in a position of strength and the worst-case scenario could mean being purchased by a competitor.

INITIAL PUBLIC OFFERING (IPO)

Once the IPO path was determined, we were driven to make it happen. But the IPO process is one of transparency, wherein you must provide the SEC with a wealth of specific details including how your business model works, how you make money, your business plans, your strategies, strengths and weaknesses, and who makes up your competition. You also need to disclose all the risks to the business. Essentially this is a complete unveiling of who you are as a company. Not only do the regulators want a fully detailed picture of your business, in order to help eventual investors understand the opportunities and risks inherent in the business, but your competitors, partners, customers, and potentially interested suitors become intimately familiar with your business model, since the SEC publishes all the documentation exchanged. This means that partners and customers can now use this information against you in negotiating future deals, competitors can strategize how to beat you in the market, while suitors, friendly or unfriendly, can decide to pursue a purchase of the company. All the above was about to happen to WEX.

Nonetheless, our strategic driving force was to move as fast as we could toward the IPO to allow Cendant to realize optimal value and gain independence for WEX. We knew we had to turn around all inquiries from the SEC within days, even if it meant working right through Thanksgiving and the holiday season of '04… and it did. The investment bankers told us there was no way we could reach an IPO until the end of March based on the normal process of exchanging information with the SEC. We told them that this was finally our chance at independence and that we were going to go full speed ahead. A normal process was not our intent. By this point we had been through so many disappointments that we would do whatever it took to gain our independence.

Our CFO, Melissa Smith, drove her group extremely hard and our chief legal counsel, Hilary Rapkin, did the same. We were working right through the holidays. Some of our people didn't even have time to go home and were literally sleeping at the company's offices. Kids were stopping by to visit their parents at the office. Finally, we had a chance to have freedom and we were not going to let it slip away. We were all very passionate about securing our independence this time. The process meant submitting our material to the SEC and then answering initially roughly fifty questions they would have for us. We'd send back our responses and they'd come back with roughly another thirty questions or so. Again, we'd submit our answers and they'd come back with perhaps fifteen more questions. This process continued until the SEC felt that they had all the information they needed. Of course, while we were doing all of this, we became well aware of two companies who contacted Cendant wanting to buy us.

One of these was a competitor, which would have created a very challenging situation. This could have resulted in major changes, potentially to the management makeup, possibly to the quality of services, to our culture, and maybe our home in Maine. In addition, a competitor will most often consolidate various back-end services to reduce expenses to help pay off some of the cost of acquisition, which can result in letting many people go.

The other possible buyer was a private equity firm where senior management could possibly cash in, in a meaningful way, if they performed and once the private equity firm sold the business. Typically, their exit strategy could be either one whereby they take you public a few years later or they sell you to another company. However, while they own you, they may take actions that can change the culture of the business, look for ways to build the business up, and/or reduce costs to enhance the bottom line in order to sell it down the road for a greater value. Neither of these two tracks looked as positive to us as the IPO, but, like it or not, we had these possible sale scenarios hanging over our heads as we were trying to complete the IPO process. So, it was a hard-driving, full-force, all-hands-on-deck effort to get this IPO completed as soon as possible.

THE ROAD SHOW

The next step in the process, after receiving the SEC's approval to complete the steps to go public, was hitting the road with the IPO road show, which we did at the start of

February 2005. We had Merrill Lynch, J.P. Morgan, and Credit Suisse onboard trying to sell us to their institutional investors like the Fidelitys of the world. We put together our forty-minute presentation, which was actually about thirty minutes plus time to field questions. We then set out on our whirlwind tour, which would begin and end in New York and encompass over seventy meetings in sixteen cities, in fourteen states, in the span of only ten days. I remember heading out of New York for San Francisco, where we landed at 2:00 a.m. and were at the first of nine meetings (three each set up by Merrill Lynch, J.P. Morgan, and Credit Suisse), starting around 7:00 a.m. After an exhausting day, we were then on a flight to Los Angeles to do it all over again.

This was just the start of a brutal process of traveling from city to city, meeting to meeting. After a while you cannot remember what you said and to whom you said it. Fortunately, we had honed our presentation very carefully and had initially presented it to Cendant senior management and then to the sales forces of the three investment banks, so they could set up potential buyers to meet with us on the road show and represent the opportunity to the potential investors. This gave them a chance to hear what we had prepared and provide us with feedback.

True to form for WEX, the possibility of freedom via the IPO actually taking place was constantly in jeopardy. We were doing everything humanly possible to expedite the path to the

IPO. We knew that our bank in Utah was a timing obstacle for the private companies to acquire WEX, since if we were going to be sold, it would require regulatory approval. It would slow the process down for such an acquisition, which meant driving to the IPO as early as possible would help our chances of securing independence. The reality was that the IPO was in question all throughout the roadshow. We were being reminded each day that we could be called off the road at any point if Cendant decided to sell WEX to one of the private companies who were pursuing us.

Along the way, we also learned that beyond the $700 million we were trying to raise for Cendant in the public offering, we also now had $300 million of debt placed on the business because Cendant would be taking a $300 million dividend. The only way for us to pay the dividend was to borrow the funds from various banks. It was not an unusual move by Cendant, but it meant we would be strapped with the debt for some period of time and it would restrict our ability to invest aggressively in our business.

The ten-day road show was a blur, but it also was a success, as the investors liked what we had to say and many were willing to put up their money, at a reasonable price. After hopscotching through cities all over the country, we finally flew back to New York to meet with investors there, then took the train to Philadelphia for the last few investor meetings, and returned to New York, unscathed. Cendant had not pulled us off the road, and at this point, on the verge of going public it would have been too embarrassing for them to do anything other than continue as planned with the IPO. In the end, Cendant walked away with approximately $1.2 billion composed of the IPO value, the dividend, and the value of a tax gross up. All in all, a pretty good tally for WEX, a company that grew from humble beginnings in Portland, Maine and flirted with disaster on several occasions before hitting its stride.

SWEET FREEDOM AT LAST

On Thursday night, February 15, we had a dinner in NYC with some of the folks from Cendant, the investment bankers, the new WEX Board of Directors, and our executive management team. The board was pulled together quickly with tremendous help from Rowland Moriarty. At this point, my body and mind were tired and I was running strictly on adrenaline and the knowledge that in less than twenty-four hours WEX would be a publicly traded company and we would enjoy a level of independence that we had never experienced.

On the morning of February 16, 2005, I awoke in the Ritz Carlton hotel in the financial district of New York. I was still very tired from the last day of the IPO Road Show, but today was the day for WEX to finally realize independence. I went through my usual routine, meditated, made my coffee, read the morning papers, and did a workout. I was then in preparation mode, getting ready to have breakfast at the New

York Stock Exchange, where we would be saying goodbye to our parent company, Cendant, while officially welcoming our new WEX Board of Directors. Of course, I would also be sharing this big event with my executive team.

Today marked a milestone for all past and present WEXers, including the management teams. I would have the honor of ringing the opening bell at the NYSE, which would signify the first day of trading for the new NYSE-listed entity, WEX.

As I finished my daily routine, I pulled open the curtains in my hotel room and there, standing proudly in New York Harbor directly in front of me, was the Statue of Liberty. Coming face to face with this symbolic embodiment of sovereignty was too much. My composure that relied on focusing on the present was lost as my emotions overcame me. The realization washed over me: today was the day that WEX was going to experience a level of freedom it had never known. I was overwhelmed and had to spend a few minutes grieving, and celebrating, all that had happened to WEX.

Finally, after composing myself, I headed over to the New York Stock Exchange where the day would officially commence with breakfast, which was held in an elaborately decorated room that included a classic old clock sporting large round separate dials for the hours, minutes, and seconds, respectively. The historical clock had been used on the trading floor years in the past. There was also a rather large, exquisite Fabergé egg from Russia.

After we ate, I thanked the investment bankers for their help on the IPO, said a few parting remarks to the Cendant representatives attending the breakfast, welcomed the new board of directors of WEX, and celebrated the occasion with my management team. Then came the moment of truth, ringing the opening bell for the day of trading, a day that, for the first time ever, would include shares of WEX stock. For a few seconds, I felt great power, as well as relief, as I rang the bell to open the (then eighty-eight-year-old) NYSE for the day's trading. I was then ushered down to the trading floor to witness the first traded shares of WXS. I still have the stock certificate framed and hanging on my home office wall, a wonderful gift from my chief legal counsel, Hilary Rapkin.

We had proven the experts wrong. They told us we wouldn't achieve the IPO until late March, yet I rang the bell at the NYSE on February 16, six weeks earlier than forecasted. As it turned out, we were fortunate that our intense drive to succeed paid off. By the end of March, the IPO market had soured and we might have been sold to a new parent instead of going public. I am forever grateful to all the people in the finance and legal departments, as well as other departments, who were relentless in compressing the time period it took to allow me, on behalf of all present and past WEXers, to ring the bell on February 16, indicating freedom at last!

That afternoon we headed from the NYSE to the airport and took a 3:00 p.m. flight back to Portland, Maine. We arrived to see signs of congratulations, balloons flying overhead outside our headquarters, and most of the six hundred WEXers all there to welcome us and celebrate our successful transition to a standalone publicly traded company. It had really happened and the reality was overwhelming for me, personally. Despite the smile on my face as the celebration was unfolding, I wondered to myself if I was even cut out to be the CEO of a publicly traded company.

My concerns had nothing to do with my confidence in stewarding the business but were more of a personal nature. I had always been an introvert by nature and when I looked around at some of the people running businesses I saw these larger-than-life, outspoken, extroverted leaders with big personalities, and I knew that wasn't who I was. I started wondering how I was going to fit into this world and wondered how I would be perceived by the investment community. But Row Moriarty, always a great mentor and trusted friend, told me that the investors were going to enjoy working with me because of my honesty and integrity. He assured me that I was indeed the type of person that Wall Street would embrace. He claimed that they preferred someone they could rely on and trust to communicate honestly. He explained that they would know I was not going to push the stock and promote something that might drive the stock price up temporarily while failing to tell them the complete facts, which could result in the stock coming crashing down shortly thereafter. He reassured me that the investors, partners, and the public at large were going to embrace me, trust me, and enjoy doing business with WEX.

So, I took that confidence into my new role as CEO of NYSE-traded WEX, and always appreciated Row's unwavering faith in me even when I was questioning myself. It was his vote of confidence and experience that reassured me that I could be effective in my new role. And he was right. In fact, five of our ten largest investors from the opening IPO are still with the company today. They're still buying and selling as the price changes with the market because they believe that we're going to be honest about the developments in the business and not try to manipulate the story. If a problem develops in the business, we're going to tell them and then we're going to work to correct it or find a way to overcome it.

Row also felt that I should take on the role of chairman and that I had earned it, but I was insistent that I would have enough on my plate in this new role as the CEO and president of a publicly traded company. I wanted to get my sea legs as CEO. Subsequently, I wanted Row to take the chairman's position on the board and I would wait for the right time to assume that role. After all the time it took to finally realize our independence, I didn't want to do anything to hurt the opportunity for WEX to thrive and succeed. So, Row became chairman at that time and three years later, in 2008, I took on the chairman's role. I was more prepared by then.

A NEW ERA FOR WEX

As you may have guessed, nobody got much work done that Friday afternoon once we flew in from New York. When we did return to work on Monday morning, there was a sense of excitement in the air. Within the walls of the company, people weren't exactly sure what the new freedom meant to them personally, or to the company overall, but they inherently knew it was somehow going to be positive for everyone at WEX. I was constantly being asked by employees, customers, partners, and the press if there was really any difference now that WEX was a standalone company. My answer was that there was no one big aha moment, but it was all about the degrees of freedom that allowed us to manage our business in a new maneuverable space, controlled by us.

The degrees of freedom included the ability to drive our culture without outside intervention, to invest in our people, to invest in our business model, to consider mergers and acquisitions, to expand internationally, to diversify our business model beyond the fleet card business, and to have the guidance and stewardship of an independent board of directors who were completely focused on our success. We were also happy to deepen our ties to Maine and secure our roots in the state.

The leaders of the state and friends of WEX were very happy for us, as it was not very common for businesses from Maine to end up as publicly traded companies. Our new freedom would result in WEX becoming even more of a community partner, and for me, as well as my team, it meant becoming more involved in the greater Portland nonprofit circles. We would try to be an example for all our associates to become more involved in their communities to enhance the social fabric of all our homes in Maine.

From an emotional perspective, on the one hand we were relieved that we were finally past this hurdle and were in control of our own fate. We no longer had to worry about suddenly being sold and having someone impact the company culture, among other things. On the other hand, we now had several concerns, including $300 million of debt to pay off, quarterly earnings calls, and the responsibility of managing the business while under the watchful eyes of Wall Street, our investors, and the financial media.

Not unlike a dog that chases a truck every day but isn't sure what to do if he catches it, you need to have a plan and be ready to take control of your fate once you attain what you want, which for us was our freedom. We were now responsible to our people, board, partners, the community, and of course our stockholders, who were all paying close attention to us. There's a very positive side but there's also the reality that you've got new responsibilities to manage and it's not all a walk in the park. We had to live up to everything we told the investors while still doing everything we had done on a daily basis in the marketplace, only now we had to do it better. And we owed a lot to the people of WEX; we couldn't let them down in any way. Our fate was now entirely in our hands.

As for the stock price, Cendant priced us at $18 a share, perhaps being a little overconfident at that level. The first trades were made at about $17.50 for the forty million shares bringing $700 million dollars in to Cendant. It took a short time, but the stock reached $18 and, although the investment bankers had to wait a little while to get their money back, we were off and running as a standalone company.

Over time, we got to know the investors very well. They'd invite us down to New York, Boston, or other locations to get to know their investment houses and the analysts who covered WEX. It all worked out the way Row told me it would. We were respected for knowing our business, not getting ahead of ourselves, and not trying to hype our stock. In fact, we gained a reputation for always being somewhat conservative, which isn't a bad thing. Row's point was that it was all about integrity. I strongly believe that the trust, value, and integrity that we brought, not only to the marketplace but also to the investment community, has paid off for us.

I'll never forget that Monday morning, returning to the office after the IPO. As I walked into the office, looking at the familiar faces and the decor, in many ways it all seemed the same, but in so many ways life had changed forever for me, and for WEX… it had changed in a very positive way.

MIDDLE ADULTHOOD (2005–2014

Chapter 8
A Time for Growth

> *Good business leaders create a vision, articulate the vision, passionately own the vision, and relentlessly drive it to completion.*
>
> —Jack Welch

PARENTAL GUIDANCE: NYSE COMPANY

After the IPO, WEX was now a 100 percent publicly traded company able to control its own destiny by making the hiring decisions, investing in the business, creating its own strategies, and acquiring new companies, all stewarded with oversight by a carefully selected board of directors. After going public at $18 per share in 2005, WEX stock would go on to peak at a high of $118 and then remain just shy of $100 in 2014, ending the year at $98 a share. We were relieved and completely satisfied that we secured our independence, created shareholder wealth, created wealth for our employees, and diversified our business model to lay the foundation for continued growth and success both domestically and, in time, abroad. Independence created a burst of newfound energy and, more than ever, WEX was able to fortify the foundation for long-term sustainability.

GROWTH: IT WAS IMPERATIVE

Continued growth does not just happen; you must find a balance between discipline and innovation to ignite and sustain growth. In 2007 we completed an investor survey to find out how they felt about WEX in various categories. Overall, they were extremely positive on questions about the core business, the financial model, management, and the reputation of WEX in the market. If there was a key takeaway that emerged from the survey it centered around the ability to sustain growth on a long-term basis and that we did not have a diversified business model. While the investors agreed that our business model was strong and that we were an industry leader, they expressed concern that WEX was considered to be "a one-trick pony." They felt this narrowness left us vulnerable to a few key forces that could have a material negative impact on our business, like the price of fuel and the economy. In many respects, they were right, but in other respects we were already addressing this concern by putting in motion the actions and strategies that would help minimize the impact of such negative forces on our business.

The investment in and emergence of our virtual card business, together with our entry into the mergers and acquisition market and expanding internationally would eventually have an impact on this perception. We were already diversifying and knew there were opportunities to take our various business operations into the international arena, which we ultimately have been doing.

A CONSCIOUS DECISION

The timing of the investor survey coincided with the paydown of the debt we took on to satisfy Cendant's $300 million dividend, which we incurred at the inception of the IPO. By paying down the debt to a manageable target level, we now had the opportunity to make decisions on how to invest in future projects, since we were not bogged down with a debt level that limited cash flow uses, much of which was going toward paying off the debt.

We held a senior management meeting where we discussed a number of ideas that would help us frame our future course, with a bias toward growth. We made it clear that we had always been a growth company and would have a principle to continue to be a growth company. However, satisfying this bias would have several implications for the business. First, we had various platforms already, and one could easily make the case to consolidate the platforms to realize efficiencies and reduce our costs. However, pursuing such a consolidation strategy would have an impact on our future growth. Our CIO at the time, who had bought into the growth strategy, made it clear to the senior team, the IT team, and the company that we would see an increase in platforms for some period of time, not a decrease as we pursued diversification, which included growth opportunities domestically and internationally.

Second, we had strong a cash flow and knew one aspect of future growth would come from investing in acquisitions, which would represent inorganic growth. With respect to platforms, we appreciated that the potential acquisitions could have unique platform requirements that wouldn't easily allow consolidation. Acquisitions could be in the form of enhancing our business model competitiveness in the North American market, either through a product enhancement or through market diversification. Acquisitions could also involve international expansion, which would open us up to new markets. Again, we knew this could also mean unique platform needs and not a quick consolidation of platforms.

Third, we had started to turn a profit in our virtual card business, and with increased investments, we could strategically expand this business model organically. The core virtual card product made an impact in the rapidly expanding online travel agency (OTA) business, and we knew for us to satisfy the demands of our current and future partners, we would need to make substantial investments. The virtual card product platform was outsourced to an outside third party, which meant another platform was supported to satisfy our growth strategy, and if we were now looking to aggressively expand and grow in this new market, platform rationalization was not going to happen in that area at the time.

Naturally, all of this was communicated in our strategic planning sessions with the board of directors, and they were supportive and wanted to see us continue as a growth company. Their experience and stewardship would be helpful as we started to navigate the various strategies we were going to pursue to build and sustain a growth course. They also made it clear that platform rationalization would need to be addressed at some point in the future or it could slow our growth down in the long term.

FROM PURCHASEE TO PURCHASER

Knowing we had five different owners after the VCs owned us and sold us, provided an appreciation of what it was like to live through the uncertainty of being acquired. This reality helped shape our process approach as the post-2005 independent WEX would now become a purchaser of businesses. From 2007 to 2013 we acquired ten companies to help fortify and diversify our business. Yet when we completed an acquisition, we did so with a keen awareness of the potential impact upon the employees and culture of this acquired company. We could look every one of each company's employees in the eye and convey that we appreciated the uneasiness of being acquired, having been on the other end of such acquisitions ourselves five times.

We knew that each and every employee wanted to know what the acquisition would mean to them personally. How would their job and the jobs of their coworkers be impacted? We made it a principle to be upfront and honest with each acquired company and their employees about our intentions. The best way to absorb or integrate a business and their people and minimize disruption to the acquired company is to be honest about your intentions. Such an approach will build trust and they will at least begin to feel more secure once the changes, big or small, are implemented based on what they were told. Anything short of that could create a moral breach with people, if the employees feel misled. This could make it challenging to execute and fulfill the mission of the business, which was paramount after investing our precious capital. Within WEX, we always treated everyone with the respect and honesty they deserved. Acquiring companies meant that we would extend that same respect and honesty to our new colleagues.

DIVERSIFICATION IN NORTH AMERICA

In North America, we were clearly the industry leader in the smaller vehicle class fleet card market, with our WEX fleet card, a host of private-label fleet card and major fleet leasing co-branded fleet card programs. But we were aware that there was a product deficiency that existed and left us vulnerable or uncompetitive in a few markets. If a fleet was diversified in their vehicle makeup, which included smaller vehicles like automobiles, vans, or light trucks, as well as heavy trucks (tractor-trailers), we were not a viable solution for that company, because of the heavy truck fleet card requirements which we could not satisfy. In addition, we observed that some of our fleet leasing partners were becoming more aggressive in expanding into leasing heavy truck vehicles to existing customers and new customers. Unfortunately, they could not satisfy the fleet card product needs for the heavy truck customers with their co-branded WEX card. This left our flank exposed with some of these diversified vehicle fleets, and potentially, with some of our fleet leasing partners.

In an effort to fill this product void in what we could offer customers, in 2012 we successfully acquired a company called FleetOne, which was primarily a heavy truck fleet card provider. They were not only accepted at the truck stops across the United States, but had the product functionality that was necessary to satisfy the heavy truck fleet card needs. This acquisition was critical because it rounded out our product set, in that we could now supply competitive fleet card services to existing or new fleets, and partners, which included the large tractor-trailer fleet card needs.

Essentially, FleetOne, which we purchased for a little over $350 million, provided strategic value for WEX in a number of ways. FleetOne's then current customer base was, by itself, a growth surge for WEX and, in addition, it opened us up to a market that we were not competitive in prior to the acquisition. They had their own fleet card platform, which was customized to satisfy the heavy truck fleet card requirements. Our CIO's prediction and our bias for growth, even if it meant having to manage multiple platforms, was continuing to play out.

On the virtual card product, we were continuing to establish ourselves as the market leader in the online travel market in the United States. We were constantly researching other markets that might be able to use the functionality of a virtual card to make large ticket payments and possibly replace purchase order and check disbursement practices. In terms of large markets that might adopt the virtual card product, we explored the health-care market where insurance companies made payments on behalf of the insured employees of their business customers to health-care providers, such as hospitals and physicians.

In the insurance market, our product strategy was for the insurance companies to replace the Automated Clearing House (ACH) payments with a more secure and control-based virtual card product. The product functionality and ease of use was an advantage for the virtual card product, but the increased cost to the hospitals and physicians was substantial when compared to the ACH payment option, and consequently, adoption was much slower than we or our partners anticipated. But what this entry into the health-care market provided was an introduction and understanding of the various payment solutions that already existed, and/or those that could possibly be created in this massive and expanding market.

Eventually, my successor, Melissa Smith, explored the health-care market further and realized that there was a B2B-based market called Consumer Directed Health Plans (CDH). This market seemed to fit our core payments criteria of being a B2B payments product and market in which we could add value by providing security, control, and information services, through partners, to companies for payment products that would be used by the employees of the companies. In 2014, WEX purchased Evolution1 for approximately $500 million. The company supplies its card products, such as a Health Savings Account (HSA), through 500 various partners to approximately twenty thousand employers and to their approximately-seventeen million employees. In this case, we took on another platform that we would have to manage, but the platform product requirements were very specific and unique to the CDH market. The goal for WEX was to help Evolution1 expand their presence in the health-care market over time by deploying some of WEX's best partner practices and by utilizing the strong cash flow of our business to enhance or broaden products, as well as consider new acquisitions.

GOING INTERNATIONAL

Over the years, we saw various fleet card programs emerge in different parts of the world, some of which had business models that were similar to what we were doing at WEX. In addition, during this time, many of the major oil companies had also implemented electronic fleet card programs in various parts of the globe. On the virtual card side, the online travel companies were also quickly expanding internationally to satisfy US travelers, and eventually, the in-country demand in these international markets that continued growing for online travel bookings. With our newfound freedom in 2005, we knew we would eventually have the opportunity to expand internationally in both our fleet and in our virtual card businesses, respectively.

The next chapter focuses on the international expansion of WEX through building, aligning, or acquiring our way into four continents with our various products and through our strong commitment to growth and diversification.

GROWTH OPPORTUNITIES EXTENDED

While WEX continues to grow today, this was a significant period of mindful, coordinated growth with several goals in mind. We had the ability to leverage our knowledge of our core products, the strong brand we had established, and predictable strong cash flows to expand beyond the core North American fleet card program that distinguished us. However, our intent and vision was to do this with a strategic road map and plan. We knew that some of the growth would be accomplished through organic investments to expand products and markets, like the expansion of our virtual card program with the OTAs and moving that product into the health-care market. In addition, a portion of the growth would be inorganic by acquiring new companies as we did with FleetOne and Evolution1 and some of the international fleet card programs.

We accomplished a number of things with both organic and inorganic growth strategies. Through the acquisition of FleetOne, we covered a weakness in our product set to fleets in North America who required a heavy truck card product, which we did not offer in the market until this opportunity arose. We were trying to build the product, but the cost was proving to be expensive and the timing of being a comprehensive supplier of services and offering broad truck-stop acceptance with our new product was proving to be a major challenge.

The expansion of the OTA market into international markets was more of a timing challenge, from a regulatory and infrastructure-based standpoint, but once we built the capability in key foreign markets, it further solidified our relationships with the large international OTAs. In a way, it was another example of overcoming a weakness, but in this case, it wasn't as much product related, but more specific geographic, regulatory-based solutions. We knew if we didn't step up and become a broader geographic supplier of coverage to the OTAs, others would satisfy the international markets and potentially vie for the US business as well.

Finally, extending our virtual card product into a new market, health-care, provided the knowledge that initiated an organic build to supply a payment option to insurance companies. Because of this entry into health-care payments, we also realized that there was an employee-based market that our virtual card could not satisfy, so we acquired Evolution1. All of this ultimately resulted in WEX building and expanding its product capabilities to open up new markets for growth domestically and internationally, as well as acquiring new companies that expanded us into new markets in North America and internationally. Since 2007, the WEX market opportunities were expanded from the fleet and OTA market in North America to the fleet and OTA markets internationally, as well as extending our payments to reach into the very large and rapidly accelerating US health-care market.

Clearly, WEX was no longer a one-trick pony, but we now found ourselves competing in new and large markets, both domestically and internationally that demonstrated a diversified business model that transformed the company into new dimensions with great growth opportunities. This diversification accomplishment also forced us to reconsider the Wright Express brand name, because research highlighted the fact that our new domestic and international markets were confused by the name Wright Express. The Express part of the name gave a connotation to many people in these markets that we were an airline, trucking, transportation, or carrier company. In addition, our associates and partners typically referred to us as WEX, short for Wright Express, and within the walls of WEX we had products like WEXsmart, awards called WEXcellence, referred to ourselves as WEXers, and a host of internal terminology using the WEX name. So for various reasons, in 2013, we officially changed our name formally to WEX and also acquired the rights to have our NYSE ticker symbol changed to WEX. The name and tagline became "WEX, We See Corporate Payments Differently." Changing the company name further reinforced a transformation of the company into a broader supplier of products in both US and international markets.

WATCH THE TRENDS AND ACT ON THEM

While growth opens up numerous new opportunities, you also have to remain diligent and constantly monitor how your business is progressing in the marketplace, and where you stand in conjunction to factors that are both in and out of your control, such as the changing economy.

In 2007, WEX supported greater than 300,000 fleet customers and we maintained data that provided trends across diverse Standard Industrial Classifications (SICs), which is the government system of classifying industries. One such trend we followed was how much fuel an active vehicle purchased on a monthly basis. Keep in mind that in the fleet business, vehicles will be deployed to service the customers as needed and their usage is not necessarily influenced by the cost of fuel. Knowing this, we kept a keen eye on the trends of our fleets and the various SIC codes to help us monitor and assess the health of the economy.

From experience, we knew the first data trend that would inform us that something was shifting in the economy was when the number of transactions per month per vehicle would start to drop. Eventually the number of vehicles being utilized for a fleet would be the second indicator to be reduced and that could foretell an even greater economic slowdown. In effect, as the business demand for service drops, the drivers will start buying less fuel. If the demand worsens, the company then starts to lay off drivers and their total vehicle utilization is also reduced.

As it turned out, in the fourth quarter of 2007, while we prepared to deliver our quarterly earnings report and call to investors in the first part of 2008, we noticed a drop in transactions per vehicle from the more typical 7.5 transactions per month to roughly 7.2 or 7.3 transactions per month. This may not sound like much, but consider how many fewer transactions this is across a total population for WEX of approximately 4.5 million vehicles.

We reported this in our report and call to investors. The investors and analysts who covered us found this a little confusing, knowing the economy seemed to be positively moving along and no one was warning of any slowdown nor did there appear to be any recession looming. We were, in fact, even met with some skepticism, but we not only reported it, we also took proactive preventative action just in case this was a warning sign of an economic slowdown.

The first thing we did was to work with an outside consultant to assess our credit and collection practices in order to minimize bad debt write-offs, especially if an economic slowdown was taking place. This was beneficial during 2008 when the financial collapse occurred that September. We were able to minimize the bad debt write-offs on a relative basis. Initially, as the Great Recession caused many companies to lay off drivers and others to close their doors, we experienced a spike in bad debt write-offs, but as the initial shock passed and companies found a way to survive, our bad debt levels returned to normal.

In addition, when the financial crisis hit and was at its peak, the large financial institutions/banks were somewhat frozen and were not easily granting credit to businesses. This paralyzed some of our competitors and their approval rates plummeted. If a competitor was managing private-label portfolios for oil companies this would become a major issue for the oil company knowing their marketing dollars weren't yielding the amount of new business they were targeting.

In the case of WEX, having the specialty bank in Salt Lake City we mentioned earlier provided us with a way to take the placements of Certificates of Deposit (CDs) from investment firms where their clients were taking money out of the plunging stock market and looking for a safe haven, such as CDs. Consequently, we had plenty of liquidity to take on new accounts and because of the work we did to tighten up our credit and collections practices, we were still able to approve over 70 percent of the credit applications submitted on the WEX card and/or on a private-label oil company card program. Prior to the recession, our approval rates were around 80 percent, so the drop-off was not that pronounced and we were chugging along while the financial markets were basically locked up. After 2008, we used this positive information to help win some private-label bids from competitors who experienced low approval rates during this time.

As it turned out, at the end of 2008 the FED announced that the recession had actually started in the fourth quarter of 2007. This was the time at which we first saw the lagging results of the fleet company fuel purchases and began taking preventative action. We used our early indicators to prepare for tougher times by making sure we could collect efficiently and effectively on fuel purchases by our fleets. We were also better prepared to approve new businesses coming through the new business pipeline because of the enhanced credit and collections procedures. In addition, our bank had sufficient funding capabilities to absorb the float required for the new businesses we were approving.

With this data, we also became more vigilant in managing the expense base in our business, and even in 2008 and 2009, this expense control together with the credit and tight collection policies, as well as still approving new businesses, helped us increase our net income. I'm proud to say that during my tenure as CEO, WEX never experienced a decline in net income. This was also something we were proud to highlight to our investors and to any prospective investors. This all helped add to our claim that we had a very predictable and resilient business model, which was borne out in the toughest of economic times.

No single indicator can predict the future, but we found that if you pay close attention to your metrics and see a trend forming, you need to be prepared to act. It is in your best interest to make plans to protect your business interests if the indicators point to the need to tighten up on your management practices and make all necessary adjustments. This may mean making sure to enact procedures to collect what is owed to you, maintaining positive cash flow and watching your expenses closely.

Some of the lessons learned during this period included being open to feedback that will prompt you to take positive action, as we did when investors indicated that they considered WEX to be a one-trick pony. This reinforced our strategy to expand and diversify the business model, so we did just that. A company should also closely track indicators in its business, look for trends (positive or negative), and listen to what investors, customers, partners, employees, and shareholders are saying that could foretell impacts on your business. And be prepared to act appropriately and decisively to positively impact your business model in the short term and minimize disruption of long-term goals.

When considering our drive to put in place various capabilities to diversify and grow the business, I am proud of the fact that in my last six years as CEO, WEX was recognized for being on the Forbes Magazine list of "America's 100 Best Small Companies." It further demonstrated the collective work, effort, planning, and execution of WEX's management and all our associates in embracing our perpetual drive to be a growth company.

Chapter 9
International Expansion

The only certainty one can count on when considering international expansion is the many uncertainties you will encounter.

After paying down the debt we were saddled with from the dividend extracted by our former parent, Cendant, during the IPO process, our business model provided us with a strong cash flow position that offered us the opportunity to consider international investments and expansion. As we considered growth avenues beyond the North American fleet card business, we were focused on international opportunities. However, we knew that trying to enter any international market without some sort of presence was a nonstarter and likely to fail.

In the fleet card market, we decided that we would either leverage our strong relationships with major oil companies to potentially partner with them in international markets, where they had a presence, or we could consider acquisition candidates that were already in various targeted geographies. When considering acquisitions, we ideally preferred to consider companies that somewhat resembled what we were doing in North America. This meant having the capability to manage the full life cycle of services in a fleet card program. Strategically, our goal was to have a "clear line of sight" to the ultimate customer, who in our case was the fleet.

We surmised that if we were steps removed from the fleets in the services we could offer in the market, we would compromise our value and consequently the economic model. If, for example, all we were supplying in services was our platform to process transactions, while the oil company had the direct interface with the fleets in the market, our value would be limited and the economic model minimized. For WEX, the strategic value we could offer was demonstrated by integrating and managing the full life cycle of a fleet card program to provide our wide range of value-added services, either through our own card or through a partner card.

The full life cycle of services included having a core processing system that supported credit adjudication, card production, fleet report production, billing, customer service and collection services, and the full acquisition services of marketing and sales. The problem was that there were not many WEX lookalike companies around the globe to consider acquiring. Over time we became aware of companies in the UK and in Australia that were mirror images of WEX, in that they managed the same full life cycle of services. They had their cards accepted at multiple major oil company brands, processed private-label cards and they provided co-branded cards for leasing companies, which was very similar to what WEX was doing in North America. Initially, the UK company owned the Australian company, but over time the two were split into two separate entities. Ironically, they were at one time both owned by Cendant, at the same time that Cendant owned WEX. However, Cendant decided to sell the UK company to a European leasing company that had a strategic relationship with PHH, along with the Australian company.

We would have preferred to combine the UK and Australian companies with WEX, but, as far as we knew, this was never considered to be an option by Cendant. Eventually, the new parent—the European leasing company—sold the Australian fleet card company, which created the two standalone entities. Beyond these two companies, there were hybrids, some of which may have provided some of the life cycle of services or had either their own card or possibly provided just a private-label product. Additionally, in some markets there might have been smaller players that provided similar services to WEX that we did not know about. There were also two heavy truck card companies in Europe that did the full life cycle, but pretty much for trucking companies only, not the smaller vehicles that we concentrated on in our North American markets. It became clear after meeting with these companies that both had some level of family ownership but were unwilling to sell the entire company or a majority interest.

In some cases, an acquisition could have also enhanced our ability to utilize the service capabilities of the acquired company to supply services to international oil companies who had fleet cards. For example, we could then bid on and supply private-label and/or co-branded services to the major oil companies in the countries or region where a newly acquired business was present. Such a newly acquired company could very well provide the servicing infrastructure in those markets.

This all sounded very logical and strategic, but as we ventured into international markets to explore the limited opportunities for acquisitions, we soon realized that servicing a major oil company in any international market would have complex challenges. In addition, the timing of executing a potential acquisition, or competing for a major oil company's private-label business, was out of our control. To be able to compete for the opportunities, if and when they arose, also meant we had to be ready and in a position to demonstrate our ability to take on the challenges, whatever they might be, especially with the servicing of oil company private-label card programs. The result of competing for such ventures is that the investments become more expensive than originally forecasted, which we would soon find out.

ENCOURAGEMENT TO GO FOR IT

Naturally, Europe would seem like the logical geography for WEX to address, because most of the major oil companies existing in North America had a strong presence in Europe. However, I was to find out that the European businesses were not waiting for us with open arms. My first endeavor to explore the European market was in the late 1990s when a few of us made a trip to the European offices of several major oil companies to discuss our capabilities and to explore potential opportunities. They knew who we were because of our success in the United States, where we were servicing many oil company fleet card programs. But these initial meetings felt a little bit like my first meetings in the United States with the major oil companies, in which the reception was a little icy and we would leave the meetings realizing that such a road would be a long and winding one.

Actually, our reception in Europe was even worse than what we initially experienced in the United States. First, we discovered that they were very proprietary and proud of their fleet card programs. The programs were not outsourced in any substantial way, as they were in the States. This alone made the discussions much more difficult since they weren't really looking to outsource to a third party at the time. But we also got the strong feeling that they were not interested in a US-based company landing in Europe and becoming a fleet card partner of any consequence. The meetings were cordial in that they were as interested in finding out about us and our products as we were in finding out about the landscape in their markets. However, that was the only common ground. They were not interested, in the least, in considering any sort of relationship with us in the foreseeable future. So we ended up taking in some local eateries and culture and had little excursions around a few countries, but that was all we could claim as the takeaways. There was no follow-up at that particular time.

Fast forward to the mid to late 2000s and a couple of new developments were providing WEX some benefits and openings to at least consider the European market again. WEX had clearly established itself as a premier provider and partner of private-label oil company fleet cards in North America, which gave us greater credibility. More importantly, somewhere in the early to mid-2000s, the major oil companies began to manage their various proprietary card programs on a global basis and not a geographic management basis (i.e., United States, Canada, Europe, AsiaPac, etc.). So the tides had turned in a few ways that made the new discussions more optimistic for WEX.

This was best demonstrated during a key meeting in 2007/2008 with a major oil company's international card manager who was very satisfied with how we had proven ourselves to be a reliable and value-added provider of their fleet card program in North America. As they discussed their international fleet card strategies, it became clear to us that if we could replicate such capabilities internationally, it might allow us, over time, to compete for some or all their international fleet card businesses. Luckily, we were in a position to begin exploring the opportunity. We proceeded to get the right parties together within WEX and with a couple of consultants explored, over a few days, what it would take to make a valid play to enter the international markets.

The key ingredient, which we recognized, and kept coming back to, was that to be successful internationally, it was imperative to have an international fleet card processing platform. In exploring the options we had available to us, we either could consider internationalizing our North American fleet card platform or finding an international platform to purchase. We quickly surmised that converting our North American platform had various risks, which included adding complexity to the current platform. Such a process could possibly destabilize our existing platform at the time and even jeopardize our North American business. In addition, working on such a massive endeavor could slow down required development for our North American fleet card businesses, which could hurt our competitiveness and upset our partners. The resulting decision, at the time, was to leave well enough alone, with respect to our North American fleet card platform, and see if we could do a worldwide search to find an international fleet card platform. We were lucky to find a consultant in Europe who came from the fleet card industry and knew the fleet card landscape in Europe and other regions of the world from his personal experience. In addition, there was recent research conducted by his firm that was specific to international fleet card platforms.

The consultant was well informed about the market and potential platform options available in the market. We worked with him and he directed us to a company in New Zealand that recently built the basic foundation for an international platform. They had built an early version, years ago, that was adopted and licensed by a few major oil companies, so they were respected in the fleet card market.

The core processing capabilities of their new platform seemed robust and could provide multiple metric, linguistic, and currency configurations, as well as very flexible product capabilities. Clearly, we needed the multiple language and metric capabilities, depending where in the globe we would try to compete for oil company business. In Europe, we knew we would have to be able to bill a fleet in their native country currency, regardless of where they purchased fuel in the European market. Our technical experts were impressed with what was presented and were convinced it was as state of the art as could be developed at the time.

We proceeded to negotiate the purchase of the platform in 2008 and also worked to hire the consultant to head up our international operations, which would be headquartered in London. The purchase price was reasonable, but we made a critical mistake in one area of assessment. As I said earlier, this platform had a basic foundation, but we underestimated the requirements to build out the platform. We were better able to understand this once we purchased it and had to start building out the capability to accommodate, and manage, a full array of servicing capabilities on the platform. The core platform needed to be equipped with a robust customer relation management (CRM) system, an accounts payable system, and a database to house the fleet data, which were not part of the core processing system we purchased. However, the robustness and flexibility of the platform did not disappoint us.

We were now able to demonstrate to oil companies the capabilities of the new platform and the feedback was very positive. Early on, we were able to secure a major oil company's processing business in one region. There were early bumps on implementation, but once we went live with this oil company it performed at or above expectations. This was proof of concept and validated the value of the platform we had purchased.

Our goal, however, was not just to be a processor, but to also manage the customer interfaces, and possibly sales and marketing. This is where we had built a reputation for high quality services in the United States. However, in Europe the initial opportunities were only to provide processing, which meant the oil companies wanted to maintain the customer interfaces and sales in-house. Remember, in the mid-1990s, we found out the oil companies in Europe were very proprietary when it came to controlling customer interfaces? It was evident that this had not really changed over time. This was probably because of the complexity of the market that had requirements to manage language and currency diversity.

The oils were interested in finding new processing platforms that could provide better product capabilities. Nonetheless, we were not successful in winning these processing opportunities. In hindsight, we are grateful that we weren't. A pure processing relationship with the oil companies would not require many value-added services and we would not have a way to differentiate ourselves. In this case (just doing the processing), "your line of sight to the customer is very removed," as we would say.

Our value is demonstrated in the fact that we can manage the customer interfaces of customer service, credit, and collections and, if allowed, the sales and marketing services. Customer interfaces may have been easier for us to adopt in the European market, but we had not developed any expertise or insights into the fleet market in Europe that would allow us to effectively take over the sales and marketing for an oil partner. More importantly, we had no customer contact centers in the market and no experience in managing the linguistic, cultural, and diverse complexities inherent in the European marketplace.

A NEW EUROPEAN OPPORTUNITY

In 2011 there was a new opportunity emerging in Europe that would require the winning partner to manage the customer interfaces as well as the sales and marketing. This was an opportunity that had not developed up to that time in Europe. As it happened, a major oil company made the decision to outsource the entire dimensions of the fleet card program to a third party. The program would be accepted at their branded locations in nine countries and they had approximately one million cardholders.

Clearly, this potential opportunity was extremely appealing to WEX, but we knew that on our own, we would not be capable of managing all the responsibilities outlined in the upcoming bid. We needed a strategy that would enable us to compete and win the business, which would include call center experience and sales and marketing capabilities. Over time, we had become acquainted with a fleet card company in the UK. They were sales and marketing experts, with a core competency of reselling fleet card programs for the oil companies across Europe. This also meant that they understood how to service the cultural and diversified needs necessary to work within multiple countries. If we could somehow combine our processing platform and customer relations expertise with their sales and marketing capabilities, we knew it would put us in a position to not only compete, but put forward a compelling combined offer that could put us in a position to possibly win this appealing piece of business.

In time, both parties got to know each other better and agreed that the opportunity was real and mutually attractive. We respected each other's capabilities and agreed that we brought complementary expertise and services that would allow us to be compelling partners to an oil company looking for a fully outsourced organization to service their business. We also realized that, individually, we lacked what the other company brought to the partnership. It was clear that neither party was looking to sell its business, so we explored other ways to combine forces. Ultimately, we entered into a joint venture (JV) with Radius, the marketing experts. WEX would own 75 percent of the newly formed JV, and the JV would initially focus on the attractive opportunity in front of us in the European market.

The fleet card business that was in play was extremely attractive to many companies that had already established a presence in the European market. Our JV offered a new, robust international platform and strong customer service expertise, along with proven European sales and marketing capabilities. In addition, we featured the combined intellectual capital of two strong fleet card organizations. In the end, we were successful at winning this very competitive piece of business in 2013.

There is another strategic nuance to this story that was a revolutionary development. In every case up to this point that I was aware of around the globe, the oil companies contracted with a third party to manage their fleet card portfolio for a specific period of time, maybe five, eight, or ten years. After that they could either renew or decide to go out for bid, and if you were the incumbent you could possibly lose the relationship and the right to manage their portfolio going forward.

In this case, however, and for the first time that I was aware of, the oil company decided to sell their portfolio and business completely. This meant the winner of the process would own the fleet customers, their receivables, contact centers throughout Europe, and the sales and marketing responsibilities. This set a new precedent that made a significant impact in the European fleet card market, which up to this time was a very proprietary environment. We were now firmly established in the European market with contact centers and a sales and marketing presence and would use this new relationship and newly purchased business to demonstrate our capabilities as a comprehensive full value partner. This may not have been the way we would have mapped things out back in 2007/2008, when we decided to expand internationally and buy the New Zealand platform, but through strategic planning and because we understood the oil company's full service requirements, we formed a strategic JV that resulted in owning a real and viable large fleet card business on the European continent.

Let me just say that there was a long gap from 2008, when we purchased the New Zealand platform, to 2013, when we signed the agreement to buy the major oil company's European operation. During this period of time, the WEX board of directors consistently challenged us on our investment strategy with respect to the platform and only having a processing relationship with one oil company internationally.

Clearly, the processing piece of business was not large enough to justify the purchase and maintenance of an international platform. Many of our board members had seen other companies, with which they had experience, attempt to profitably enter the European market, and they were not always successful. So, knowing the risks, they were justifiably skeptical and concerned. They were always looking for an update and any positive development. On top of that, the investment community kept questioning our European strategy, so we had to be cautious in what we said. We knew there was no guarantee of success, and there were many days where we questioned the strategy of what we had taken on and wondered if it would ever materialize into a viable and profitable diversification strategy or if it would end up as a failed market entry attempt.

Winning this large fleet card piece of business, in many ways, was not only validation, but there was also the potential that this could lead to further strategic opportunities in the European market over time. Remember, early on, it took us eight years to turn a profit in the base WEX fleet card business in the United States and five years to turn a profit in our virtual card business model. Therefore, I was confident that we would find a way, so we never gave up hope. I remain confident that over time we will see WEX develop a meaningful presence in Europe and I will feel proud of the vision and contributions that I, and others, made to that success and presence.

PERSISTENCE PAYS OFF

In the mid-1990s, I also became aware of a fleet card program in Australia that was owned by the UK fleet card company, referred to earlier. From what I knew, the business model seemed to have followed the track that WEX had followed in North America. They had their own fleet card accepted at most oil company retail locations, they processed for a few of the oil companies on a private-label type of product and also had relationships with some of the fleet leasing companies in Australia. They appeared to resemble WEX in many ways, just in a much smaller market.

As mentioned earlier, the UK fleet card company that owned the Australian business was eventually purchased by a major European fleet leasing company that had no leasing business in Australia and didn't want to continue owning the fleet card business down under. My understanding is that it was sold to a company called Retail Decisions. Somewhere along the way, Retail Decisions (ReD) had employed a CEO who at one time had managed the UK fleet card company that also owned the Australian fleet card company.

I had met the CEO when he was still running the UK fleet card company and we continued to meet periodically thereafter. When the European leasing company decided to dispose of the Australian business, the CEO of Retail Decisions was able to acquire the business. I stayed in contact with him and WEX even used ReD's fraud-based card product for our fleet card business in the United States. ReD, was a publicly traded company. Sometime in the mid-2000s their stock was put in play for purchase by another company. With our history and knowing their stock was in play, we put our hat in the ring to buy them. The result of this process was that the management team of ReD found a private equity company to team with management to buy ReD's stock and take the company private. I was told by the CEO that WEX was their second-best option for the management team, but at that time this offered us little solace. We would remain patient.

Then in 2010, the private equity company that owned ReD decided to split off and sell the Australian fleet card business, Motorpass, via a process open to other bidders. We ended up being one of two finalists vying to win the business. Naturally, the private equity owners were interested in maximizing the sales price and their return. The management team, we were told, was in favor of the business ending up with WEX. Their influence wouldn't trump the price, but could have an influence if we were competitive. After satisfying almost all the private equity company's requests, including a competitive price, and negotiating a purchase and sales agreement, we felt compelled to put an ultimatum date on our completing the purchase.

Some of this was done because we believed they would try to leverage us against the other suitor to extract a higher price. So, on a Thursday, I instructed our M&A team to communicate an ultimatum that we wanted to sign the purchase and sale agreement by Friday or we would extract ourselves from the sale process. A rumor arose that the other suitor was flying down to meet that coming weekend to offer a better price and attempt to displace us from winning the business. We never knew if this was true or not, but I concluded that we had done everything asked of us to complete the sale and if we didn't draw a line in the sand, we could wake up on Monday and be told we needed to sweeten our bid or we would lose out to a competitor. So, we made the demand on Thursday and waited.

By midday on Friday there had been radio silence and the feeling at WEX was that they were not going to honor the ultimatum and the opportunity would be lost again. But at around five o'clock that Friday afternoon, we got the phone call we were hoping to receive. They called to say they were signing the purchase and sale agreement. WEX became the proud owner of an Australian fleet card business, one that very much reflected the strategies of WEX and one we had watched patiently over time.

The acquisition of Motorpass in Australia did a number of things for WEX. It made our entry into the international market substantial and viable, which created new opportunities for WEX employees, both at the headquarters to manage this new entity and for those who wanted to volunteer and relocate down under. It also signaled to the investment community that WEX was investing to diversify our business geographically, which had a positive impact on our stock price.

The acquisition also became an entry point into the Asia-Pacific market. At the time, it was the largest acquisition WEX had ever done, over $300 million. Keep in mind this was 2010, so behind the scenes, we were still working to justify the New Zealand platform purchase and the long road to entering the European market. Two very different paths, but opportunities present themselves in different ways and at different times. The key is being able to be nimble, which translates into being able to respond to market forces as they materialize. I also believe our reputation in all the developments was a soft, but real, advantage that helped us when the decision by the various parties was between very competitive bids.

BUILD, BUY, OR ALIGN

In many cases, you have to determine how you will proceed to diversify and expand your business. Diversification or expansion can be accomplished by *building* new products that are complementary or adjacent to current products or by *building* the requirements to expand into new markets within your current geographies or into new geographies. Another option is to *buy* companies that provide you with diversification opportunities in current markets or new markets, even geographic markets. A third possibility is to *align* with another entity to enable expansion of the business and tap into the expertise of the aligned partner. WEX would deploy all of these diversification strategies.

For us, the acquisition of Motorpass in Australia was clearly a *buy* scenario. The entry into Europe included a *buy* component, which was the platform purchase, but it also involved an *align* strategy that culminated in the JV that ended in the buying of the oil company portfolio. On the *build* strategy, we found that our virtual card product required us to expand our capabilities on various fronts to satisfy the needs of our online travel agency (OTA) partners that are providers of hotel bookings worldwide. Remember that WEX became a worldwide virtual card payment provider for the likes of Priceline and companies that managed the secure payments to hotels that were booked by consumers through the OTAs.

The OTA virtual card program represented an emerging innovative product finding its way into new markets, but up to that time, we weren't successful in finding acquisition candidates or a partner to align with to help build out the international requirements for these partners. This is primarily a result of WEX being a first mover in this market, where we ended up competing with large banks and American Express, neither of which constituted acquisition candidates or joint venture opportunities for WEX. As we scanned the international markets, we quickly realized that there was a lack of viable acquisition targets that would accelerate our entry into the foreign markets. In this case, WEX has been successful at expanding internationally by *building* the capabilities to utilize our virtual card product competitively in multiple countries around the globe.

In Brazil, we found an employee benefits provider of B2B payroll/debit cards that also had a fleet product for heavy trucks and, we believed, could enable us to provide a solution for establishing our virtual card program in Brazil, and possibly other South American markets. As it played out our business venture turned out to be a hybrid solution. First, we *aligned* as a partner, purchasing 51 percent of the company in 2012 to form a joint venture, allowing WEX to enter this new market. Then, in 2015, we *bought* the remaining 49 percent of the JV and we now own the company outright.

The Brazilian JV was a way to enter a new geography where in-country expertise and stewardship helped us enter the Brazilian market in employee benefit card programs, where we might be able to assist them in expanding their services in this market. In addition, we now had the opportunity to explore how we could bring our fleet card expertise and help them expand this part of their business. It could also help WEX build out our OTA program in that country and region. It was very helpful having a motivated JV partner to help us expand and build on three products in a new geographic territory for WEX.

By 2016 we would have a physical operating presence in sixteen countries and do business in more than thirty-five countries worldwide, with over 2,000 employees in force. We understood the fundamentals of the businesses we acquired, and went through a learning curve to attempt to integrate relevant parts of our culture into each country's business and social makeup. By dealing with partners and customers in these markets, with our acquired or integrated products we quickly became aware of the differences of the cultural environment. But we had to make sure our core values were being blended or reinforced in their business culture. More than ever, we needed to create trust in those instances, and never be so arrogant as to think that how we do things in the United States would be easily adopted by our business partners abroad.

From our experiences establishing our presence overseas, we recognized that there is no single formula to pursue expansion of your business, especially internationally. The key is to consider all the options of build, buy, or align and to understand the tradeoffs as well as the pros and cons. Market expansion opportunities offer ways to diversify your business and potentially enhance growth prospects, but they most likely will have time pressures and resource and capital requirements that must be carefully weighed and assessed before making any commitments. Be prepared to make mistakes, especially when it comes to timing expectations. If you create a vision, together with thorough strategic planning and understanding of the landscape, it will go a long way to minimizing major failures and write-offs.

Chapter 10

Culture: Adapting for Continued Growth

You have to work consistently to engage the hearts and minds of your people to become a force for strategic advantage.

Throughout the book, we have talked about the various stages of development that WEX went through and the cultural developments that we tried to create and reinforce to define ourselves. In a B2B business model like ours, the relationships you forge are considered strategic relationships, with deep integration of services between both parties to provide greater value to the market.

Think about providing private-label fleet card services for the likes of Sunoco, ConocoPhillips, Sheetz, Quiktrip, ExxonMobil, CITGO, and many other companies that have spent years and innumerable expenses creating a brand presence in the market. Then consider the fact that they integrated their fleet card programs with WEX to provide the key value-added services and products on their proprietary fleet card in the market. Clearly, they had to implicitly trust that we would not damage or detract from the brand image or the goodwill they diligently created.

195

Through the years, and continuing today, we have constantly had partners communicate to us how real the engagement and investment that our people, at every level, demonstrate in working with them and their customers is. They tell us that many companies talk about how important culture is, but at WEX they could clearly feel it and see it.

Even our board members have commented to me that they enjoy having board meetings at WEX because as they walk into the building they begin to feel the energy of the place, which speaks to our associates and their emotional investment in driving the business forward. People at WEX are proud to be part of an organization that respects them and respects all our stakeholders. This is not just about the sharing of our values on a piece of paper, but it is about how we consistently conduct ourselves in a way that reflects the respect we have for each and every partnership we have entered into with these large and successful companies.

WEX embraced the fact that we could develop a culture that became a strategic advantage that helped propel our success. Our partners trusted us to provide the highest quality products and services so that they could be competitive in the fleet card marketplace. In prior chapters this was highlighted when we discussed how we rewarded the "What and the How" a person demonstrated in their work to move the company and the culture forward. We rewarded those who found ways to satisfy our partners and who enhanced and secured such important partner relationships.

While taking pride in the culture that emerged throughout our years at WEX, we also knew that there could be cultural aspects that, if not addressed, could hamper the trajectory of future growth. We had to be careful and make sure the stated needs of our partners, and our willingness to satisfy those needs, did not become detrimental to WEX in some regard. When we made the conscious decision to strategically design the business to drive growth on a long-term basis, it meant more than diversifying the business and model; we also decided to explore our cultural framework to make sure it would support and optimize this growth goal. Our intent wasn't to fundamentally change who we were or what helped get us to that point. We knew that our culture was a driving force in our success, and we had to be careful not to fundamentally alter this strategic advantage.

Our culture had a core competency of partnering, which was fundamental with our distribution partners and the fleets, but eventually was extended to our associates, and even the community. But we realized that there were aspects of our culture that might need to be adjusted to better accommodate growth in a larger, more diversified WEX. At least, that was our intent when exploring the full makeup of our culture and how it supported and/or hindered us in driving our long-term growth strategy.

Fortunately, in the past, we had done some work with a local company that had a global reach and an understanding of business dynamics, especially the role of talent and culture.

In 2008, we engaged with Rand and Associates to explore a cultural realignment of WEX to better support the drive for sustained growth in a more diversified business model. Rand educated us on how they divide cultures into four major classifications: Control, Competency, Collaboration, and Cultivation. They basically mapped these four classifications onto a quadrant chart. In each of the quadrants they would place one of the four Cs identified above.

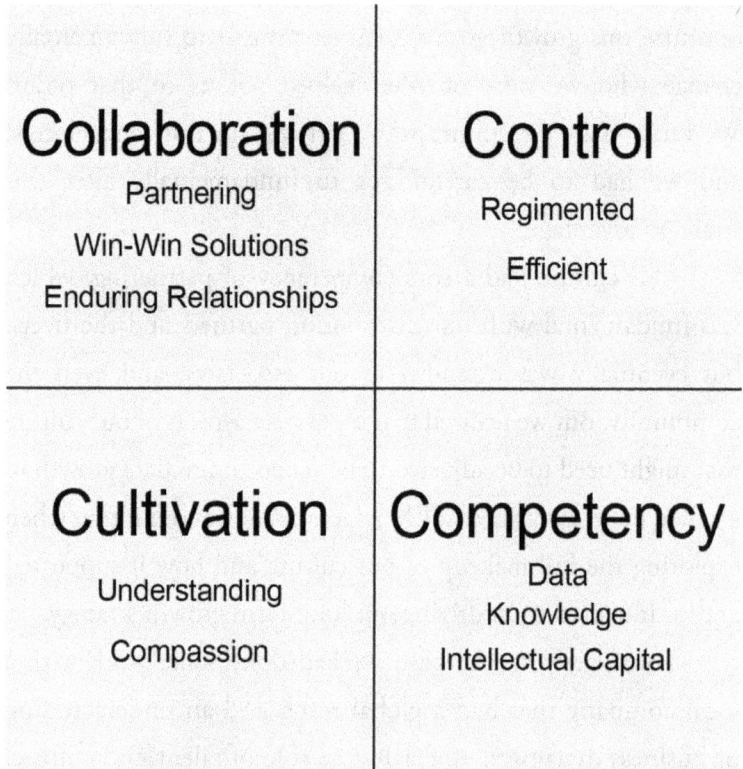

Collaboration	Control
Partnering Win-Win Solutions Enduring Relationships	Regimented Efficient
Cultivation	Competency
Understanding Compassion	Data Knowledge Intellectual Capital

Control represents cultures that are very regimented. The military is an extreme example. In business, it may be evident in a company, such as UPS, which needs to adhere to a very statistically based regimen to manage their business model efficiently and effectively. A Competency-based culture places a lot of emphasis on data and knowledge to drive their success. They know what it takes to succeed in each aspect of the business, they know their competition inside and out, they know their own strengths and weaknesses, and they value intellectual capital. GE has been mentioned as a company that represents this category of culture. In a Collaborative culture, businesses strive to partner with their customers to find win-win solutions to build long standing relationships. WEX adopted many of the attributes of this cultural leaning. And finally, in a Cultivation type culture, organizations attempt to allow for relationships to be enhanced and strengthened through understanding and compassion. Typically, nonprofits are the types of organizations that are represented here. Rand communicated to us that every business has some of the attributes of each culture category, but typically, a company will take on key attributes of two of the categories, with one being dominant. Within each of the quadrants the more you are on the extremes of the quadrant, and away from the center, the more an organization primarily takes on the attributes of that type of culture (e.g., the military as a Control culture), and the more you move toward the center of the quadrant map, the less you take on the depth of the attributes of a particular culture classification. Through our work with Rand, we determined that WEX was both a Collaborative and Competency-based culture, with Collaboration being the dominant cultural basis.

We recognized that each of these categories also have detrimental aspects, especially if taken to extremes. In the case of Collaboration, we discussed how we became a collaborative dominant culture, which manifested both internally and externally into our behaviors. Internally, we found that we had moved toward a consensus-based decision-making company. This resulted from our efforts to give everyone a voice in shaping company policy. In such an environment, you start to realize that there are numerous people in meetings representing so many stakeholders within the company. They are all trying to make decisions, and any one stakeholder has the power to say no to a request, which means there is no consensus and the decision to move forward can be stymied.

For us, this became very frustrating at times, in that overriding a no decision became problematic. For one thing, if we decided to move ahead on a change without a consensus, it could disenfranchise the parties who were against the decision to change and move forward. We knew this had to be changed. While we wanted the process to continue to have sufficient input from various stakeholders, we also believed that a decision should still reside with one or two key stakeholders and not have to be consensus-based.

In addition, with respect to our partners and our external decision making, what started to set in was that it became harder to say no. There was concern about satisfying the collaborative relationships that had been nurtured. The ongoing willingness to say yes to partner demands starts to result in customization for many of your partners, and if you think about that, it can slow down the ability for a company to manage all of this individual-based customization. More importantly, by saying yes, the weight of customization across many partners can eventually slow the growth of taking on new business. It became apparent that when a partner asked for a special tweak to our products or service practices, we would, within reason, say yes. In most cases, these requests seemed to make logical sense to improve the product or service, but may not have been necessary to meet competitive conditions in the market. In effect, we were customizing because of a special request, not necessarily based on sound or required market conditions. While this was happening on a regular basis, we were also soliciting new partner business opportunities. They might also require some reasonable level of customization for us to take over their current fleet card portfolio.

Even in the sales process, our sales reps might be saying yes to special customized requests that weren't necessarily market-based requirements. So, with limited capabilities to do it all, we might end up finding ourselves in a position to have to arbitrate between satisfying a current partner's request or being able to satisfy a new partner's needs that could be required to win their business. The result could be added expense to do both, or, if we couldn't manage both requests simultaneously, we could find ourselves disappointing one of the parties, or worse, not win the new business.

As mentioned earlier, we were also rewarding our people who advocated for our partners' and customers' customization requirements. We concluded that WEX was, in many cases, finding itself in this situation, and if we valued growth, we would need to find a way to shift the culture more toward Competency as a dominant trait, while still retaining the key positive attributes of Collaboration. In doing so, we would need to find ways to soften the extreme behaviors of not having defined boundaries, saying yes too often and routinely customizing, all of which could limit growth.

What we realized was that we needed better data and information in order to focus the resource efforts of our people and our investments on what the market truly valued and what our competition could offer. This would result in less customization and provide us with better data to explain why customization might not be necessary. But in order to do that, we needed to develop the capability to do deep market research on what the competition was doing or providing in the market, as well as research that provided WEX with a better grasp of what the market truly valued. This spoke more to a Competency-based culture and would allow us to factually defend why we could not say yes to every request and why we weren't providing customization whenever our partners or customers thought it was needed.

One such example involved pricing the cost of fuel based more on a wholesale price indicator than the retail price of the fuel embedded in the pump price. This was usually a private-label fleet card request, which would mean not charging the fleet for the pump prices, but instead changing the fuel price based on a wholesale price benchmark. To a commercial account, this seemed reasonable since they felt like their price should not be similar to what a consumer would pay, but tied more to a wholesale price index.

Having done more research, we were now able to point out to the oil company partners that, even though the wholesale price plus mark-up and the retail price might vary day to day, during any extended period of time (thirty, sixty, or ninety days), the prices tended to average out and are roughly the same, assuming the oil company wanted to maintain the same margin on fuel sales. And if the oil company wanted to provide a discount to the fleet, our system already allowed them to offer a discount off the retail price. We could reflect the retail price, net of the discount, on the fleet's bill. By showing the oil company the data, and the reasoning behind it, we were able to refrain from having to build this new and complex pricing mechanism into the product. Whereas, in the past we might not have used the market data to show them that the fleet would not save any money on such a transaction versus the retail price once averaged over a period of time. Subsequently, we might have agreed to customize the product, while now we could explain why it might not be necessary.

Despite our new-found emphasis on research and data, we were not going to abandon the core attributes of Collaboration as an integral part of our culture, since it was clearly what set us apart as a partnering organization. Therefore, in order to optimize growth, we concluded that we would need to strive to be more Competency-based in our cultural framework, while sustaining Collaboration. Making this happen, though, would take a disciplined strategy and vision to actually reshape our current deep-seated cultural attributes. Working the strategy and processes with Rand would hopefully provide a sound road map of how we could achieve this reshaping.

The plan we put in place with Rand was that they would assess all the VPs, SVPs, EVPs and me to determine each person's critical thinking capabilities and how each person was wired as a manager at WEX against various management attributes. This was followed up by a 360 review exercise to determine and confirm the manager's capabilities, and hopefully, reinforce the assessment that Rand completed on each manager.

This baseline provided an understanding of our overall collective leadership capability and how we fit into the current WEX cultural framework and what it would take to change the status quo to better meet our new shift toward Competency.

Rand then put together, with the executive management team, the leadership attributes that we would value in our current and future leadership, which would embrace more of a Competency-based culture.

These attributes would support greater strategic and innovative thinking, using data to help determine decisions, knowing the capabilities of the competition, knowing the market needs, basing decisions more on quantitative inputs versus qualitative inputs, and valuing intellectual capital when it came to understanding the depth and breadth of the business and our markets. We would then separately build these attributes into our evaluation process for new employee hiring, development and training of current employees, evaluation/compensation processes for employees, and succession-planning practices. If executed successfully, it would result in us hiring new employees who were better prepared to satisfy these attributes.

Putting training and development programs in place would enhance the attributes we were striving to embed in our management teams and culture. In our motivation/compensation practices, by evaluating and compensating our management in their yearly evaluation process against the attributes they were to model and manage, we hoped to start to change the behaviors of our managers. Finally, we would begin assessing our leaders for succession opportunities against the criteria we were now embracing to define our culture.

We tried to have our managers continue collaborating with our partners and/or fleets, but also begin to research and use the data we could make available, to make financially sound decisions with the partner's input. This meant our managers who had an impact on product or services would now need to listen carefully to why a change was requested from a partner or fleet and basically say, "I will get back to you," rather than "Yes, we can do that." In the new environment, the manager had a responsibility to WEX and to the partner to bring to bear the data and research that determined what real impact such a product or service modification would have on the fleet experience. This sort of behavior needed to become the norm for WEX in order to better manage partners and customer expectations. It also made financial sense to WEX, in both the short and long term. The bottom line was that this cultural realignment would better support growth in a more complex and diversified WEX, which we were fundamentally embracing.

These changes would not be easy, but we were at least systematically putting management practices in place to shift to a cultural framework that favored a Competency/Collaboration-based culture versus the past Collaboration/Competency-based culture. It meant that if we adhered to our new management practices, we would now hire employees who embraced the new realigned culture, and we would develop our management team with a bias toward those attributes. We would then reward managers who showed the capability to embrace these cultural values, and we would be preparing managers to move, over time, into more responsible positions within WEX. At the end of the day, if we were diligent and successful in implementing these changes, this would all contribute to the culture favoring Competency, but still retaining key Collaboration attributes.

As a company develops in its formative years, its cultural attributes are also formulated and become reinforced and ingrained over time. But as the business evolves, and hopefully grows and diversifies, management may have to step back, reflect, and ask this question: can the current culture support the future goals of the business or is a cultural realignment necessary to better meet those goals?

We strongly believe that, in our B2B business model, our culture has been a strategic advantage for our success and we were careful not to compromise that advantage. Our goal was to realign the culture so we could compete more effectively to satisfy the demands of our valuable partners, both current and new. We had recognized that the current culture, if left intact, could impede the growth trajectory that we were envisioning. So, even though the previous chapters focused on our conscious decision to diversify and have a strong bias toward growth, we knew that to maximize growth opportunities, we also needed to make sure we had the management tools and capabilities to drive a culture that would better embrace and enable growth in a larger, more diversified business.

Chapter 11
Retirement: A Tough Decision and a Tougher Process

The only way to make sense out of change is to plunge into it, move with it, and join the dance.

—Alan Watts

I recall a specific meeting with my eventual successor, Melissa Smith, back around 2007 while conducting her annual performance review. During the review discussion, we talked about what she wanted me to consider for her future roles and responsibilities, and as a career path within WEX. At the time, she was the CFO of WEX and was continuing to distinguish herself as a leader in the company. In my mind, I could conceive of her potentially being considered to succeed me someday, when the time came for me to transition out of my role as CEO. What I remember, and what surprised me, was that she made it very clear during that meeting, without me prompting the discussion, that she wasn't interested in being the CEO of WEX. She told me then, "I would never want your job. It is too lonely." Little did I know, at that time, that she would end up being my successor. However, following that meeting and for some time, it became a key concern for me as I moved closer and closer to the reality of retiring as CEO.

Fast forward a couple of years, to a meeting I had with the vice chairman, Row Moriarty, who asked me if I would determine approximately how long I would consider continuing as CEO. He felt it was only fair and critical for the board to understand my expectations, so we could all plan the course and changes well before the actual time was determined. So, around 2009, after careful introspection and consideration, I provided the board with general, nonspecific guidelines on my timing to remain as CEO of WEX. I said I wasn't exactly sure but it was possible that it could be in the next four to six years, depending on a number of internal WEX and external factors. It would mean that I would be around sixty three to sixty five years old when I would possibly transition, assuming the plans were successful in finding a suitable successor to take the reins and guide this wonderful company to new heights of achievement, the timing for the company was suitable, and I was actually ready.

However, at the time, I also questioned the possibility that one of the potential candidates for my job, Melissa, might not want to step into such a role. Such a lonely role, as she had stated earlier, wasn't of interest to her. I realized that if she wasn't really interested in the CEO role, it could have an impact on how we might eventually play out the plans for succession. Regardless, this did not change my mind in regard to the timing of my transition.

SELF-EXPLORATION—DON'T TRICK YOURSELF

People sometimes wonder why I decided to transition and retire from running the business that had become a big part of who I was as a person. Everyone knew that WEX was my cause and probably didn't expect that I would be contemplating such an early transition from running the business in which I was so invested. Some expected that I might have to be physically extracted from the business, while many could not even conceive of WEX without me. WEX and Mike Dubyak had become somewhat synonymous. My wife, Denise, thought I should seriously consider researching how others had planned their transitions in order to make it a positive experience for me and for all who would be impacted by the change. She was concerned that upon leaving, if I hadn't thought it all through and planned it properly, I might go through some major withdrawals and find the transition extremely challenging. But the reality was, when I assessed what had been accomplished professionally and how long I wanted to continue driving myself, as well as what I wanted to do later in my life's journey, I knew I was ready to start the planning process for my transition. A number of considerations contributed to me setting the possible timetable, with the board, at a four- to six-year transition plan.

To everyone's surprise, including mine, it became a smoother transition for me than anticipated. But like so many situations in life, if you properly understand the nature of the circumstances and put the time in to planning out the various scenarios and impacts that could arise, the chances of a successful outcome are improved. Many influences contributed to my ultimate decision on timing. I have tried to capture a couple of the major ones that probably helped reinforce, or solidify, my decision.

Since the loss of my father, I was always driven to succeed, which meant I was a man on a perpetual mission. I can look back on what I was like as a child prior to my dad's death, when I was ten years old, and after his death. Up to that point, I was a little hellion and my achievements in school were not very promising. After his death, there was a marked change; I went deep inside and became very serious, not wanting to burden my mother in any way. This defining moment in my formative life, I believe, was the source of a strong drive that had two wellsprings. First, even though I may have shown some athletic capabilities as a youngster, once my dad died and the aforementioned changes occurred, I also became obsessed with the pursuit of athletics, which is still a passion of mine, even if it is now more as an observer. As a young man, sports became a way for me to express myself nonverbally, and even though I wasn't aware of it at the time, a way for me to bring honor back to my family. Second, perhaps in a quest for order that had escaped my life up until that point, I became internally and personally focused on a drive for perfection.

When reflecting on it as I got older, I realized that I had the proclivity to have order in my life and have things be as perfect as possible. This is typical of a person who was raised with the dysfunction of an alcoholic parent and wants to control those things they have direct control over, because there are bigger forces in your life that you cannot control as a child. Quite frankly I found myself realizing, in my forties, that this personality trait would limit my ability to grow as a leader, and I became focused on overcoming the bias to do things myself because I thought I could do it better than others.

I was aware that if I could not trust others who worked for me to take on more responsibility, I would limit my capability to grow as a leader of larger organizations. Over time, I worked hard at putting in place various practices that could help me in this pursuit to grow and take on more responsibilities. By making it clear to people what was expected, laying out the milestones to track progress, and providing a feedback loop to discuss progress, I slowly became more comfortable delegating. More importantly, I realized that in my competitive makeup, the fire that existed wasn't so much driving me to defeat my opponents in athletics or business, but was instead an internal compass that had me constantly challenging myself to be the best I could be. This led me to take on more and more goals, because I believed I could develop my skills to reach, and then surpass, what I determined was necessary to succeed. When I assessed a situation, whether it was on the athletic field or the business arena, I would size up the opponent or the challenge and believed I could develop myself to eventually have the ability to accomplish what was required to succeed or win. When it came to athletics, it was essential to develop the skills to win and progress. It didn't matter if I was in little league or playing basketball all during high school and college, I would emulate older players, even the pros, and believed I could develop my skills to do the things they were doing at their level.

I had to work hard on the practice courts or fields to perfect my abilities, but there was this confidence that by doing so I would meet or exceed the standard I had set for myself. Sometimes when it came to business, in all honesty, I put myself out on the edge, occasionally perhaps too far. I had to summon all my capabilities and thirst to learn so that I would not get so overwhelmed with the challenge that I would fail. I believed in my capabilities to develop the necessary skills to the point where I would sometimes take on a challenge before I was truly ready. This often required me to work feverishly to manage through any adversity while trying to avoid major blunders that might result in failure. I was hardest on myself whenever I didn't succeed at something or didn't do it fast enough. It was not a destructive self-flagellation, but more of a disappointment in my preparation and I would quickly try to surmise what I could have done differently.

I was constantly reading self-help books to develop my personal capabilities and core makeup as a person, as well as business books that were all about being an effective leader. When an opportunity arose, I just couldn't hold back. This was especially true when I took on the role of president and CEO of WEX. At least four of the prior CEOs of WEX had run larger organizations prior to joining WEX and never seemed overwhelmed with the WEX challenges. They brought with them their own developed management styles and philosophies, which may or may not have served them well at WEX. Nevertheless, it didn't seem like the challenges were over their heads. But I had never run an organization with its full array of management requirements, especially one like WEX, when I took the reins in 1998. The broader role required someone who could develop and refine the internal disciplines to support a dynamic and high growth business, which was also in a very challenging place with over 40 percent of the people looking to leave the company, even the senior management. The burden to manage through so many challenges was compounded by the fact that the other experienced senior managers were leaving and I would need to rely on less experienced internal successors and/or newly hired management that would enter WEX and have to first experience their own learning curve in order to understand the business model. Only then could they help me curb the exodus of our associates and drive the business.

I was comfortable with the external challenges required to drive the growth of the business, since I had taken a primary role in helping to build and develop strategies and relationships over the years. However, it took me a couple of years to get my sea legs squarely planted under me and feel like I was on top of all the challenges that developed or had been served up to me as a new CEO. But I was now in the CEO seat and I was the one who had to find a way to navigate through the challenges effectively.

Throughout my career, I cannot think back at any major business failures, which may be why my innate confidence found me continually taking on challenges that put me out on the edge. This is not to say that I didn't find myself, many times, with setbacks that required me to learn from my mistakes or from the situation and move forward. I knew from early on that setbacks in business, or in sports, were part of the learning process. Even those challenges that could have materially harmed the business, if not sufficiently addressed and corrected, were methodically managed in a way that found us by the early 2000s in a very different place. The culture had become a strategic advantage, loyalty and associate satisfaction for WEX were reflecting best practices, the infrastructural issues were being addressed, the external market dynamics found WEX achieving high levels of success and the management team had developed and jelled into a dynamic and very capable group of leaders.

Another effect of the sea change of my youth was that I strove for financial stability because I saw my father broken by his failures in business, which ultimately put his family's security in jeopardy. I realized in my twenties that his failures had become a driving force in me, and the reason why I never wanted to let my family down or find myself financially broken, as my father experienced. So, when assessing where I was in my life and my career, it became apparent, when I took a step back and reflected, that I could feel proud of my business accomplishments, as well as achieving financial security.

The next step in planning my succession became a personal exploration of what I felt was best for my wife, Denise, and me. Did I want to remain at WEX for an extended period or was it time for me to move into another phase in my life? I had been at WEX since 1986, experienced so much and felt that I had accomplished a great deal. The demands of the business would only get more challenging, and I needed to be honest with myself in order to determine if I was up for it. I had put my heart and soul into the business to push, plan, strive, and drive for its success. Now I needed to take a hard look inward to make sure I still had the motivation and the fire in me to continue.

I want to reiterate that meditation provided the grounding for me to be in touch with, and assess, my life's expectations and desires for fulfillment. My conclusion was, if I could properly orchestrate a positive transition that would satisfy all the relevant stakeholders including the board, the WEX associates, the shareholders, my wife, family, and me, I was ready to methodically pass the baton and start to direct my retirement as CEO.

I was fully aware that such an orchestration wouldn't be easy and that there were forces beyond my control that could interfere with my plan of making it seamless and successful. For example, what if the economy took another major nose-dive and WEX would need to dig out and push through the challenges for the business? Clearly, I would have postponed my retirement plans. There were various other scenarios that could have arisen that would cause me to stay on longer than the four or five years that was then in the plan. But I knew I had to concentrate on what I could control, to put my plans in place and execute them.

There is no doubt the business became a big part of my identity, but for various reasons, once I began exploring the pros and cons of retiring, I was able to do it in a detached manner that was not swayed by my emotional investment in WEX. I believe my ego has always been in balance and has not defined or blinded my life's path. This is probably because I have been meditating since 1975, which I initially embraced as a way to increase my energy. I soon found out that it had so many other benefits physically, mentally, and emotionally. It created a centering and balance of my being that has kept me grounded. I like affirmation of a job well done, but don't need to be in the spotlight or feed off ego-supporting accolades. Remember, my confidence that came from my internal competitive nature created a strong confident inner self, so being successful for me was expected. Let me be the first to say that in life and business we will encounter failures; the key is not to let them paralyze us or deter us from learning from our mistakes. We must accept failure and continue to move forward.

This expectation created a little bit of a problem for me in that, when I achieved something or the company achieved something, I didn't do a very good job of celebrating that success. I think this was because I assumed I would make the goals a reality and then would just keep on moving to the next goal without looking for a pat on the back. To better understand my behavior, I remember back in the early 1990s, the president of WEX at that time had me work with an assessment firm that put me through a battery of tests to assess my psychological and mental capabilities. They concluded, at the time, that my ego might not have been suited for the role of CEO, because I was too understated.

During the assessment, I had a discussion with one of their consultants that would have an impact on me and change my thinking about striving to be understated. When they asked me for quotes that I adhered to or believed in, I mentioned a particular quote that says, "The whale only gets harpooned when it spouts." I discussed my interpretation of this quote as meaning that if you are too boastful, you open yourself up to be hurt or harmed in some way. The consultant said, "Well that's true, but another way to look at this is that the whale needs to spout to live." I took this interpretation to heart and realized I might need to put myself out there a little more and not be so understated that it could hinder me, give anyone the wrong impression, or hurt the company in some way.

So, out of all this work, it was apparent my ego needed some healthy exposure. Part of my inclination for not wanting to be in front of people, internally or externally, was how hard it was as an introvert to just be out there doing anything that required me to stand in front of people making speeches, or for that matter, doing any kind of public speaking. It was, however, my drive to succeed at WEX that meant I would have to find ways to overcome the hesitations and fears of being in the spotlight. Leading by example might work on the athletic field, but I was realizing it wouldn't work in this business setting.

A leader in business needs to be somewhat more outspoken and publicly accessible. Without making this change and seeking out more exposure, I could find myself in a place where my ability to grow and take on more responsibility would be severely compromised. That was not an option. There's no doubt I wasn't the most comfortable or polished speaker early on, but I continued to work at it and over time felt more comfortable and confident, which is the key to becoming a better speaker.

Once I decided to transition and step away from my CEO position, it wasn't a weaning process for my ego that concerned me. Quite frankly, once I realized I didn't need to keep achieving at such a competitive pace, I experienced a slight lack of motivation, which I knew wasn't fair to the people of WEX.

They say once you start to emotionally step away from your job, your commitment isn't the same. I knew my commitment to WEX and to myself wouldn't let me coast to the finish line, so I maintained my focus on detail and remained dedicated to moving WEX forward. But when my transition was completed at the end of 2014, I was sixty-four years old and had been with the company for twenty-nine years, so I was more than ready to move on.

No matter when I retired, the company would always be progressing, and with a company predicated on growth, the demands of the business would continue to increase. Upon my retirement, WEX had operations in five countries with a host of European operations soon to be added, and the international travel had become very demanding and physically draining. Travel had lost some of its luster and was no longer something I looked forward to doing, but I had accepted the fact it was necessary. I think the demands of international travel were really reinforced when, in 2012, I traveled with Melissa Smith, who was then the WEX president of the Americas, to Brazil to welcome the employees of the joint venture partner, UNIK, which WEX had entered into in Sao Paulo.

This is how the four-day and three-night journey played out. We boarded our plane in the United States on the evening of day one and slept on the plane during the eleven-hour flight. We arrived early in the morning on day two at our hotel, found our rooms and, after some much needed showers to wake us up, headed to the UNIK offices. Upon arriving, we had an agenda already set up that would have us first meet with the president of UNIK, then his management team, and, in the afternoon, the one hundred-plus employees to discuss our plans and welcome them aboard as part of WEX. However, during the meetings, we were receiving information on another acquisition in the United States that had taken on a life and timeline of its own, unbeknownst to the UNIK employees.

Due to the confidentiality agreements and insider information guidelines, we could not discuss this transaction in any way with the UNIK people. The new developing acquisition would end up being our largest at the time ($350+ million). It was a business owned by a private equity group who insisted on closing the deal while Melissa and I were in Brazil. As much as we wanted to cut the Brazil trip short to concentrate on this very meaningful and large acquisition, and the steps to close it out, we knew it could come across to the people at UNIK as disrespectful.

So, we remained in Brazil and had to work the process to close the deal while meeting with, and welcoming, the UNIK teams. While Melissa and I were in Sao Paolo, we had to review certain closing documents that required WEX board approval during the first evening. After hours of reviewing documents, we were finally able to sleep in our hotel beds, which was a welcome luxury after sleeping on the airplane. On day three, we conducted a WEX telephonic board meeting to approve the US acquisition. Then we met for the last time with UNIK management, before working with our communication department to get ready to conduct an investor and analyst call during day three to announce and explain the substance and synergistic rationale for the deal. This was done in a hotel conference room, where we lost hotel phone service twenty minutes prior to the investor call and I ended up making the call on my cell phone while our CFO, who was in Maine, joined me.

The investors had no idea I was out of the country and that the CFO and I were not in the same room conducting the meeting. Thank goodness for technology and an uninterrupted phone connection. Then we boarded a plane later that night and had the "luxury" of sleeping again on the plane on our return to Maine. I got to the office on day four after the overnight flight, hit the WEX showers, and changed clothes, before I went upstairs to the conference room, where investors were already assembled.

One of the financial analysts, who covered WEX, had invited about a dozen of their firm's institutional investment clients to our WEX headquarters for a meeting. When it was initially planned, the meeting was to be a general update of our business activities and had nothing to do with the new acquisition that was just announced yesterday. The timing, however, was such that the new company acquisition would be the main focus of the meeting, especially knowing it was our most expensive acquisition to date.

So, in the course of four days and three nights, two of which meant sleeping on a plane, I met the employees of a newly acquired joint venture company in Brazil, consummated our largest acquisition to date, met via conference call with our board and investors to explain the rationale for the transaction, and had a face-to-face meeting with current and potential investors at the WEX offices. All of this helped reinforce my decision to stay on a course to transition the business to another highly motivated leader who could bring a new level of motivation and energy to WEX.

Besides the demands of running WEX, there was another major factor that influenced my decision. I had met a most captivating woman. I had gone through a divorce, which was very difficult for various reasons and left an emotional toll on me. The last several years of my first marriage were challenging both with my ex-wife and my daughter, and I was emotionally raw. Then into my life came Denise. I met Denise a few years earlier through a WEX associate at a WEX-sponsored event; beyond our meeting there was no further interaction.

Then, one day in 2003, during my separation from my ex-wife, I noticed her, in passing, at the Portland airport. I tucked away the thought of maybe finding out, sometime in the future once some time had passed and I had worked through the emotions of ending a marriage, if she was in a relationship or not. Lucky for me, several months later, I found out she was not in a serious relationship and I reached out to her to see if she'd like to meet.

Once we started to date, I began to appreciate how her positive emotional energy and her compassion for others were so very nurturing for me. Her playfulness helped me reconnect with the child within me who had been emotionally shut down since my dad died when I was ten years old. The playfulness that emerged helped my demeanor, and being with her rejuvenated my emotional well-being. She was also a business executive and could relate to my business challenges and was a voice of inspiration and reason when I needed support and guidance. We began traveling and fully enjoying life together when I was outside of WEX. We both loved exciting and challenging adventure travel. We have been to Alaska, Belize, Mexico, Cuba, the Galapagos, Patagonia, Peru, Kenya and Tanzania, Antarctica, Arctic, New Zealand, Bhutan, and the Colorado River in the Grand Canyon. We like to hike and enjoy the beauty of a place, the people and their culture. So, when I started to realize that life is short and you cannot take anything for granted, especially your health, I decided I wanted to enjoy life in a way I couldn't by continuing the pace as CEO of WEX. I was pleased I could make this happen and spend more time with Denise.

My family has always been important to me. I have three older sisters, with numerous nephews and nieces, as well as great-nephews and great-nieces. I have been fortunate enough to have one of my sisters, with her son and daughter, eventually move to the Boston area. The daughter has two boys. My other two sisters found their way to move to the greater Jacksonville, Florida, area. Between two nephews and a niece there are also two great-nephews and two great-nieces living in Florida. When my mother died in 2007, I decided I wanted to be closer to these two sisters and their families. None of us were getting any younger. So, in 2008, I purchased a condo in the area and began to visit during the winter holidays and for long weekends, where I was able to work out of my home office. Having retired, I now spend about half the year in Florida and more time with my family members there. Now I enjoy having two great homes where I can also be closer to my entire extended family and am more present in their lives.

My daughter, Iva, is now thirty-two years old and we have a great relationship. I look forward to visiting her in California on a regular basis or having her visit Denise and me in Maine or Florida. Iva and I have an appreciation for nature, physical activity, and spiritual exploration. I'm able to see her more often, spend quality time with her, and even offer advice on her life's experiences, when she asks. She has a writing degree, which allowed some collaboration with me on this book where she has been a great help. By reading the book, she has gained a better appreciation of my career experiences, and I have enjoyed the challenges she has posed to me to be more expressive in how I share and describe the insights discussed in the book.

My wife, Denise, has two wonderful daughters and two delightful grandsons; I'd like to believe I play a part in their lives as a stepdad and step-grandfather. The young grandson likes to spend alone time with Denise and me at least twice a year for about a week at a time at our homes. He is a true joy.

I am grateful for the health and happiness I have in my life, but I know through experiences with friends and family that life is unpredictable and fragile, at times, and I wasn't willing to press my luck. Denise and I not only enjoy being with each other during the fun and exciting times but also when doing daily routine types of things. I decided I wanted to spend more time with my lovely wife, companion, and best friend. I also have more time to be with my daughter and my extended family members, which was not so easy when I was working at WEX.

LOAD THEM UP AND TEST THEM

So, with all of this as a backdrop came the motivation to continue my path toward retirement. I had surrounded myself with talented and capable people who knew the business, bought into the culture, and were helping me drive the business successfully. Together, the board and I put a plan in place to determine if there was an internal candidate ready and capable to replace me and take the reins at WEX, when the time came.

At the time, we decided there were two candidates internally that could potentially be ready, at some point, to assume the role as CEO of WEX. We decided that one way to test their mettle would be to increase responsibility to these two top executives to see how they would respond and perform. No matter how much we loaded them up, it would never constitute the responsibilities of the CEO role, but we would try to give them more responsibilities overtime to see how they would respond. One was Melissa and the other was a sales leader who had made it clear to me, over time, of his intention to be my successor. At the time, around 2009, both had been with WEX about twelve years.

When I decided to promote them both to executive VP positions, it was with some trepidation. I knew the promotion would signal to both of them that they were now possibly in a position to succeed me, whenever that day came. They had no idea of my timing; only the board had a possible indicated timetable for my retirement. However, my last conversation with Melissa about the possibility of being CEO was not an encouraging one and I had major concerns about her desire to be my successor when I started on the path to promote and load them both up with greater responsibilities.

I remember meeting with her and laying out my plan to promote her to EVP. I was cautious and concerned that she would understand the implications of the promotion and in some fashion, maybe reiterate her reluctance to assume the "lonely" role of CEO. She surprised me when she accepted the promotion with great appreciation and committed to taking on this added responsibility with passion and energy. I knew she was smart enough to understand the implications of the promotion and was, therefore signaling her commitment to work toward the possible succession, whenever that was going to happen and if she was chosen.

The other leader also understood the implications and was grateful and energized to assume the added responsibility. I had two capable candidates for succession and it was now up to them to distinguish themselves over the next few years. As it turned out, both were successful in taking on more responsibility, but over time it became clear that Melissa was able to continually distinguish herself with each added challenge. She gained greater respect with the board, with management, the associates and our partners and customers. One aspect that distinguished her as a prime candidate for being my successor was that cross-functionally within WEX she was trusted and respected as a leader. She also was someone who wasn't afraid to challenge me, which never bothered me because I trusted her core values and openness and, consequently, respected her insights and opinions.

At the time of my announcement to transition out as CEO, Melissa was president of the Americas and the other candidate was president of International. Once promoted to take over as president and eventually CEO of WEX, I knew she would create her own shadow at WEX and not stand in mine, which is how it should be. She continues to build her own stature and respect within the company and outside of WEX, and it is easy to support all her efforts and strategies.

The other executive was disappointed about how things played out. Two years earlier, when I made Melissa President of the Americas, he was reporting to her, and that may have been difficult for him. At the same time, I hired an outside executive to be president of International, which only compounded the situation for him. He could have perceived that he was now the number three person in terms of stature at WEX and may have realized that his expectation of someday becoming President of WEX might not happen, especially knowing that Melissa was now his boss. Knowing his desire to be my successor and realizing it did not seem inevitable, had to be difficult on him. Eventually, the International President left the company and I promoted the sales executive to President of International and that seemed to re-energize him. He was back in a position of being one of the two senior people reporting directly to me and managing one of the key segments of the business. He took on greater responsibilities and proved himself worthy. However, once Melissa was announced as my successor, at first he seemed supportive, but once I transitioned and Melissa took over as President and CEO of WEX, he eventually resigned.

THERE'S NO GOING BACK

I remember being at a meeting with three board members who were working with me on my transition management structure and compensation in preparation once I decided to transition. We were getting closer to the time when I was going to decide to transition and I would need to start some level of communication, when appropriate, within WEX to begin putting the pieces in place to execute the transition plan. One of the board members reminded me that once I decided to move forward there would be no going back as we started to open up the planning process. Without hesitation, I said I understood and would be ready. I had done the work and realized the magnitude of the decision for me and for WEX, and was prepared to get the wheels in motion. A good friend of mine, Bill Ryan Sr., the former CEO of Banknorth, and then TD Bank, would remind me that the only thing people would remember about your career is your last year, so make it a positive one.

Well, truth be told, you don't have complete control over all the circumstances that impact a business and its results in any one year, but I was fortunate to hand the reins to Melissa with the company enjoying great success financially and in its diversification strategies. There was a solid foundation and platform for future success on which she could build. The transition was smooth and without any major disruption to the business. To this day, she continues forging her own pathways of success, which is reassuring and satisfying to me personally. WEX has been a labor of love for me; it almost feels like it was a child I wanted to hand over to someone I was confident could continue to nurture it, and to distinguish this great company.

By the way, in 2014, Melissa became pregnant and had to step out of the CEO day-to-day role for a short time. I was asked by the board to step back in to work with Melissa to help guide her ship without trying to disrupt, or deviate from, the path she now was charting. People would ask me, "Now that you are involved again in helping to manage the business, do you miss running the company?" Based on the above and my ease of transition, I let them know I would be happy to see her return and resume her role. Even my wife was surprised at how seamless my transition to my retirement had been.

Today, I am chairman of the WEX board, so I am still involved in the company, but the day-to-day resides with Melissa. My role managing a board whose primary purpose is to help steward the company on behalf of the shareholders is very different than that of the CEO. But from this somewhat removed standpoint, I can observe, with pride, the continued success of the company.

THE NEXT CHAPTER

Planning, acceptance and a smooth transition made it easy to step into the next chapter of my life. When considering what to do next, I received some good advice on what to focus on with my newfound free time, which had been a scarce commodity in the past. The advice was to be very careful not to overcommit as opportunities come along, because it could take a long time to unwind and work your way out of these commitments. I was now in the enviable position of being able to honor my time and only fill up my schedule with projects that I was passionate about and which still allowed me to enjoy a more balanced life. I didn't feel compelled to start saying yes to too many opportunities. I became very discreet and picky about what I would commit to doing.

I feel a real connection to Maine, its beauty, and its people. I discovered at WEX, and within the community, the depth of character that exists within the people of Maine. It is sincere and the people are genuine. I wanted to give back to the state in ways that could truly make a difference. Truthfully, the state has its problems, transitioning from a natural resource–based economy to a human capital–based economy. But the decline of the natural resource–based jobs has outpaced the new jobs created in the new knowledge-based economy. Consequently, the state sees many of its best and brightest young adults having to leave the state for careers elsewhere. As a result, we now have the distinction of being the oldest state in the country. This is a recipe for disaster down the road. Maine is in the position of having to support an older retired population and maintain the physical and social infrastructure, while well-paying private sector jobs continue to decrease. To combat this trend, I feel the state needs strong educational programs to keep its best and brightest in the state, and to help propel companies in the state to thrive.

I was instrumental in getting six other Maine-based CEOs to fund a computer science initiative, Project>Login, to close the talent gap in the computer scientist field in the state. It began in 2010 and after doing the exploratory work, eventually launched in early 2013. Today, the initiative is producing great results among higher education organizations throughout the state including the University of Maine System (USM). We were even recognized by the White House for a select TechHire program in 2015. The Project>Login initiative eventually found a home with a new organization that was the result of a merger with a K–12 and a higher education program, respectively. I became the first chairman of this new organization, Educate Maine, and today serve on the board.

I was also asked by the Chancellor of the University of Maine System to be part of an executive advisory committee to help oversee an initiative to determine the feasibility of combining the UMS law school, business schools, and Muskie School of Public Policy into a single school under one roof. This initiative, if implemented, would create a new combined school of distinction in a new building in or around the beautiful city of Portland. I'm also cochairing an economic initiative, called FocusMaine, which launched in 2016. The vision is to increase the number of high-paying jobs in the state in a select number of traded sectors that will enhance the economic prosperity of Maine. Consequently, my focus has been to direct my efforts toward helping the state I love while turning down other opportunities, which included joining public boards.

I chose to move to Maine thirty years ago, and it is apparent that the state has been a very positive experience for me and for WEX. I am emotionally invested in Maine because I want to see this great state provide opportunities for the next generation and be an attractive place for WEX to be headquartered and offer our people and their families a better quality of life. Between chairing the WEX board and being involved in these three initiatives, I'm probably at a place where I'm not looking to take on more outside endeavors. I'm busy, but very protective of my time and my flexibility. Some people have inquired if I'm interested in a political track, but I truly believe I can make more of a difference with the initiatives I'm committed to than if I ran for political office. In addition, I'm really not sure I would enjoy the life of a politician, and the time commitment would be overwhelming.

Row Moriarty referred me to a book, *The Hero's Farewell: What Happens when CEOs Retire*, by Jeffrey Sonnenfeld. I highly recommend the book to any high-level executive, especially a CEO, who is considering, or going through, a transition or retirement from a powerful role. The book outlines four archetypes and how they react to the transition and the relinquishing of the stature, prestige, and power of the role they are abdicating.

One of the most aggressive archetype is the "General" who is someone who will not easily give up wanting to direct or provide direct feedback on how things should still be done in the company. They have to be, literally, dynamited out of the company and/or the board because they are so disruptive.

On the other end of the spectrum of the four archetypes was one framed as the "Ambassador" who carefully plans his or her transition, executes it in a smooth process, and then moves on to other interests which occupy them physically and mentally. I believe that with all I have discussed in my approach to the transition, this archetype seems to fit more than any other. I imagine that Row and the board's experience is that they've seen some transition plans that went smoothly and some that did not. I think they would agree the transition at WEX has been a very fluid and uneventful one, where the business continues to move forward with a strong leader at the top.

I believe the lessons learned for any CEO who is looking to retire or transition to the board of a company, has to be one of assessing, planning, and execution. Clearly, as a CEO, a person has held a position that offers stature, prestige and power. Once you get used to that position, you must be able to assess when and how you will go about relinquishing the role. Once you know that you, or the board, are ready for a transition, you must be very honest and introspective in regard to what is about to happen.

I encourage reading *The Hero's Farewell* to get a good sense of what will play out and how your associated archetype will manage through this major change. The magnitude of the inevitable change needs to be realized, or you could find yourself second-guessing yourself along the way or regretting how unprepared you actually were to take on the change. But once this decision is made by you or for you—and I hope the change is something that you have some control over—thoroughly planning the transition is critical.

It is vital that the transition be a positive experience for all the key stakeholders and not one that diminishes the business in any way. Such key stakeholders include the board, investors, management, associates, partners, customers, the community, and the press. To pull that off will require you to think it all through carefully and, remember, that in many cases you have a limited ability when it comes to how to include various stakeholders in the planning.

In my case, it was only the board and I that knew of the projected possible timetable and who could consider the actions required prior to any finalized transition timing. Beyond that, for a publicly traded company like WEX, it could trigger a material event in which people would possess insider information and could use the information to their advantage in deciding to buy or sell WEX stock. A leak of such insider information could then trigger immediate communication to be shared with every other stakeholder and could prematurely alter the course and speed of the transition. The company might find itself managing some level of damage control instead of an orderly transition plan if anything was not ready to be unveiled.

Finally, the execution of a well-thought-out plan is critical; it may need to include some contingency planning in case circumstances change significantly. For example, an economic tsunami of some sort, or market crash, could require you to postpone the transition until the business pushes through the disruption. It could involve a major loss of business that might change the plans and the timing of any changes. You might also have a situation in which one or more of the successor candidates doesn't achieve the level of success that evokes enough confidence for you and your board to promote them.

In some cases, one or more might leave the company or make it known they are not interested in the position. Let's be honest, in many of these situations you may have very little control of the circumstances and possible disruptions, which again speaks to the level of planning that must be considered, which includes having contingency plans. I truly believe the board and I did a commendable job of planning and executing the transition at WEX, but we all would be the first to say that we had some degree of luck that nothing went off the track for us in the years building up to my declaring my actual timing, which triggered the announcement and actual transition of authority.

It has been almost three years since I retired as CEO and, on so many fronts, the transition has been a positive experience, I believe, for all parties involved. The board had a critical responsibility to manage a smooth transition of CEOs, which they can feel good about. The shareholders, who are primarily concerned that their investment in the WEX stock is not harmed or compromised in any way during the transition and that the successor create confidence in the future attractiveness of the stock, seem to be pleased. The associates and management also wanted a seamless transition and to be able to believe in a bright future for the company and their role in the company.

On all accounts, this has been happening. As CEO, Melissa clearly needed to feel supported, and not in any way second-guessed, when she took on the position of running a diversified, international growth company. In our discussions, she acknowledges that our relationship is working for her. For me personally, I have my new and different connection to WEX, which has been positive, knowing I don't have the intense time commitment that a CEO bears, but that I am still involved at the board level. Just as importantly, I have control over my time in a way that I haven't had during any part of my working life to pursue other passions and interests in which I truly want to invest my time. I also want to spend the rest of the time with my partner, Denise, to pursue our special experiences and just enjoy each other's company. I know I can only control so much in my life, but I'm grateful for to have health and happiness while sharing my life with a partner with whom I enjoy spending my time.

I like to believe my positive transition has been influenced by the fact that I was able to leave the CEO position as fully and gracefully as I did because I finished what I started out to do at WEX. Along with a committed team, I helped grow and build WEX to a place of success, where it transcended what many had seen as limitations, but I did not. WEX has achieved independence and realized perhaps its greatest potential, becoming a sustainable company that people want to continue working for, which is in capable hands and continues to benefit Maine, the state I love. Paralleling that, by watching what the company needed, pushing myself to develop as a leader, overcoming my own shortcomings, I think I became the leader the company needed, at the right time. My true cause was the company, its people, and the state of Maine. It wasn't about ego, a list of accomplishments, or staying in a position of power. I was able to leave when I did because I developed into the leader I needed to become and brought the company to its own positive fruition before turning over the reins to the next generation of leaders.

On a personal level, my life partner could see me for who I am. With her encouragement and support, I could now live my life beyond WEX: being adventuresome, launching new projects and initiatives in Maine, and spending more time with my family. When I put my head on the pillow every night, I have no regrets. I am grateful for what I have and look forward to enjoying the next chapter in my life. I sincerely believe the road for WEX will continue to be exciting and successful. I am proud of the efforts and contributions I made to this great company and am proud of all the committed WEXers who helped build this dynamic business

Chapter 12
A Unique Road to Success

Now that you have read the story of WEX, and how the company grew from a family business spin-off in Portland, Maine to a publicly traded International corporation, I would like to offer up what I believe are some of the key ingredients to driving a successful business model. The truth is that each business must drive and navigate its own path to success. I do not think anyone has a tried-and-true formula that universally fits all businesses, so it would be impossible to determine one set of pathways that can serve as a template to success for any company.

In the previous chapters, I have tried to convey the three key ingredients that had a major impact on WEX: parental guidance, physicality (product & markets), and culture. Clearly, how any company, small or large, structures its parental corporate governance and ownership will have an impact on the short-term and long-term stewardship of the business. So, when conceptualizing your vision of the company well into the future, think through what parental makeup will best support the various stages of growth, even if that means there will be changes within the parental makeup, over time.

When thinking of the physicality of the business, everyone needs to do their homework to understand the market needs and recognize how your products and services will fit into that market, and how they will be affected by future, evolving market forces that will, in time, shape your particular space. The more you dig deep into understanding market forces, the more you can optimize your ability to win in the markets you are targeting.

Finally, the culture of a business determines your company's personality, which will need to be embraced by your employees and by your targeted market. If your employees truly embrace your company culture, it will extend to your customers and have a major positive impact on your success. Don't underestimate the power of this ingredient. Do the work to determine what sort of culture will help define your customers' perception and willingness to recommend your products or services. Then put in place the hiring, development, assessment, and promotion management practices that support the people you need to drive the culture.

These are a few of the fundamentals that can help drive the success of a business, but there are so many other dynamics that will come into play:

- Whether you are in a business to consumer (B2C) or a business to business (B2B) marketplace
- Where you fall on the spectrum of a transactional product-offering relationship (e.g., selling a consumable consumer product) all the way to a strategic product-offering relationship (e.g., WEX)

- Whether your go-to market will be a direct path to the customer, or whether you will use distributors or build a hybrid model

Each of these dynamics, as well as others, may have an impact on what sort of parental makeup will be best suited for your business, and what cultural attributes will best embrace your business model market needs.

While there is no specific formula that will assure success, I will attempt to highlight five key drivers that helped WEX on its road to success and may also be applicable to most, if not all, business models.

1. BRICK BY BRICK

If we start with the premise that most businesses are in it for the long term, we can then use the Three Little Pigs metaphor on how best to protect your business from the unexpected circumstances that will, at some point, arise and challenge your business life expectancy. Consequently, it is imperative to build your foundation and your house, brick by brick, to withstand the fierce headwinds that will be encountered at some point, by economic forces, market disturbances, unexpected internal challenges, or competitive threats.

One of the first bricks to put in place is strong leadership. To minimize disruption, you'll want to have the right leaders in place, in all the key disciplines of the company from early on, if possible. These should be leaders that buy into your vision for the company and will help you build the business. Engender a team environment that rewards the "what" and the "how" of driving the business forward.

Also in the course of building the foundation, you'll want to develop recognition and reward programs that acknowledge those who are driving the business forward, but do it in a way that enhances the behaviors that you believe will best support the cultural attributes. Build the culture based on trust and integrity so that people can feel safe expressing themselves and knowing that the customers and all associates are being treated with respect. Such a culture should also be transparent and even reward transparency, as much as possible. People do not like surprises, so work hard to minimize them.

Another fundamental aspect of building a company is strategic planning. You can begin by infusing an annual strategic planning process that has a balance between outside and inside forces that impact your business model. In your strategic planning, know where you are currently in your market, determine what the opportunities are in the market, and then decide how you will deploy your resources and capital to address the opportunities, short term and long term, that will help drive your business forward. Determine milestones to track your progress and build on the process yearly. Make sure you have a principle to be bold and strategic versus being too conservative and incremental. There must be a balance in the planning process to allow for practicality in addressing the day-to-day demands of the business while also allowing for innovations and leapfrog strategies.

Creating and nurturing an innovative culture, discussed below, can prove very beneficial when forces outside of your control threaten to "blow your house down," as in the Three Little Pigs metaphor.

At WEX, for example, if we were experiencing severe economic stress, having new parents owning us, seeing new major entries into our market, people deciding to exit the company, or major partners questioning their decision to go with us, we were still able to withstand the pressures. All of these situations were encountered successfully and the shocks were absorbed because we were building our business, brick by brick, so that no one major traumatic event derailed our forward progress. I would task any business to be thoughtful in how you want to build your foundation for long-term success, regardless of uncontrollable forces that will, sooner or later, be encountered.

2. INNOVATION CULTURE

An article written years ago resonated with me with respect to building an "innovation culture." The article contended that an innovation-based culture produced more innovations than companies that primarily relied on research and development (R&D) spending to drive innovations. This is not to say the innovation cultures did not also spend money on R&D. However, these companies put in place two key components that created a successful innovation culture.

First, a company needs to support a customer-centric culture. A business must understand the needs of the market and the customers they serve by both gathering data from interacting with customers and from an outside compilation of prospects and market needs. This outside compilation of needs can be identified through sales meetings and research.

Once compiled, the data needs to be saved and utilized to help determine the incremental advances the business can put in place to increase value to the customers. In addition, your research can provide you with a sense of forthcoming market needs, so that with some innovative thinking you can create a product solution that has not yet been identified within the market. While they may be hard to come by, such innovations can leapfrog you ahead of your competitors.

Second, a company must then be committed to following through on the stated and perceived needs of the customers and market by investing in product and service enhancements. Ideally, this becomes a regular and consistent part of how a company deploys its capital: to build and introduce new products and services into the market, to both retain existing customers and become more attractive to new customers.

All businesses that want to become, and remain, market leaders should strive to be consistent innovators. I sincerely believe the best way to do that is to make innovation a cultural bias and to be willing to make the smart investments to demonstrate to the market your company's ability and willingness to step up to the changes occurring on a regular basis.

3. KNOW THE MARKET DYNAMICS

Many new business owners realize the significance of landing a lighthouse account, which they can then use to validate their business model. It is such validation that can then become a beacon to attract other companies to sign on, knowing that a respected industry leader is now using the product or service.

The path to signing a lighthouse account has to be thoughtfully considered and calibrated. You must also know the right level of lighthouse account to target. If a business believes in its product passionately, but targets a lighthouse account beyond its capability to influence and attract, they may find themselves spending an inordinate amount of time and money focusing their efforts to sign one such large and influential customer who may not be a feasible candidate at the time. To rely primarily on landing one of these accounts could become a fatal flaw in the business model. While it may be possible in some cases to "buy" one of these accounts by offering them a first mover price break or by offering enhanced services at no or little additional cost, such a strategy may not be feasible depending on your product margins.

In the case of WEX, there was nothing we could have done within our means to land a major oil company as a lighthouse account in the early years to validate our business model and crack the chicken-or-egg dilemma. We would have surely run out of money pursuing the major oil company market. After researching the market, we quickly realized that the major oil companies were inquisitive, wanting to find out more about our product and services, but we also realized that they were not looking to work with us since they possessed, at the time, the capabilities to develop their own proprietary fleet cards. Spending our time pursuing and waiting for them to say yes to WEX to develop a private-label fleet card for them, or for them to agree to accept the WEX fleet card, could have been a fatal flaw for us.

Instead we took a different route. Our market research uncovered the fact that the midsize oil companies, that were usually quicker to try new things, and who did not have their own credit card processing centers, comprised the right level of the market for WEX to target. As a result, we approached this market, and had great success. These midsize companies gained the benefit of our fleet card technology and were able to quickly introduce proprietary fleet card programs.

Meanwhile, they helped us establish ourselves in the market. No single midsize oil company could have provided the critical mass to make us profitable, but combining several of them made possible our profitability. In addition, and most critically, they gave us the opportunity to solicit and sign small fleets to our fleet card product, which validated the fleet need in the market. All of this progress eventually led to the signing of major oil companies, which propelled our success. But if we had blindly pursued a path to only focus on the major oil companies in the beginning, we would have certainly run out of money and most likely would not have emerged as a force in the fleet card market.

So the lesson learned is to know your market and calibrate the best way to validate your product entry and eventually be able to sign the relevant lighthouse accounts that can propel your business. In other words, don't try to fight above your weight class until you have established yourself in your industry.

4. OWNING UP TO YOUR MISTAKES

A business is similar to a person in that there are many relationships built over time. To build enduring partnerships or relationships, we all have to admit when we are wrong or acknowledge when we make a mistake. In both cases, we do not want to make mistakes a practice, but if they do happen, we need to own up to the reality. If we try to spin it some other way or try to put the blame on the other party, without merit, we jeopardize the longevity of the relationship. You may be tempted to pull out the contracts and try to use the legal process to distort the reality of the situation to minimize any short-term expenses for remedying the problem that was created. Or, instead, you can admit your mistakes and get all parties in the room to find a way to collaborate and work toward a solution to the problem.

In the case of WEX, we were able to admit our mistakes on some major conversions of fleet card programs and convey our commitment and willingness to make it right. We demonstrated an all-hands-on-deck commitment and worked tirelessly to minimize any disruption while correcting the problems. It literally took the better part of a year to completely remedy the situation, but by acting in good faith, we found that over time our partners recognized and appreciated our commitment and slowly we were able to restore confidence back into the relationships. Ultimately, years later, when it came time to renew the contracts, we were rewarded for our efforts and signed long term contracts with these major partners.

This lesson touches upon integrity and building a long-lasting and enduring relationship based on trust. Clearly, no one wants to find himself, or herself, facing costly mistakes in their business. But taking responsibility for your actions, no matter how painful it may seem at the time, could restore the trust in the relationship and possibly even strengthen it. Alternatively, if we breach the trust, repairing it may be impossible, and at some appropriate time, the relationship may dissolve and have little chance for future reparation. As Dov Seidman professes, "If you live up to your commitments, 99 percent of the time you win."

5. A MAN'S CHARACTER DETERMINES HIS FATE; THE SAME CAN BE SAID FOR A BUSINESS.

In business, I believe a company's brand strength is primarily determined by the emotional investment clients place in embracing the products and/or services offered by the company. The goal is to consistently strive to deepen the investment clients and other companies make in their relationship with your company.

Completing a sale of the product is only the beginning of a relationship. The strength and depth of the relationship will be determined by consistently meeting and exceeding current and future expectations of your customers. Internalizing and buying into this reality compels a company to strategically plan its products, service delivery, supporting culture, parental stewardship, management makeup, and its associates' engagement in a very thoughtful way. I like to believe that WEX consistently strives to find this portfolio balance.

Underpinning all of this, I believe that the best way to achieve a strong brand is to build your company fundamentals on integrity and trust. Research shows that if your people feel that integrity and trust, which results in their satisfaction, your customer satisfaction levels will be high as well. Unless it comes from within your company culture, you cannot successfully market a veneer of integrity and trust; people simply will see through it and not buy it. It must be demonstrated by a company's actions day in and day out, in good times and, crucially, in challenging times.

Overall, people will pay for value, and part of the value proposition is composed of reliability and trust in the company's products and services. If the character of your business is trusted and relied upon by the markets you service, you will absolutely deepen the emotional investment that customers and other companies place in their relationship with your company. This will optimize the value of your business.

I am proud of my contributions to WEX, which became more than a job or a career path; it became my business cause. Why did WEX become a cause for me? I had already convinced myself that hard work would be my path if I was to be successful carving out a meaningful career. But my career at WEX offered me something more that fueled my passion and made it a cause. While I followed through on my commitment to work hard to realize a successful career, I also had the opportunity to be creative and innovative in applying my experience to a new and exciting vision and business model that could revolutionize a market need with new technologies and value-added products and services. It was energizing to know I was being offered the opportunity to find creative pathways to synergize multiple components and forces for success. This multifaceted challenge, as it began to play out, showed incremental levels of progress toward fulfilling a vision that I helped create. It intensified my personal drive to fulfill this bold vision and the accompanying challenges.

In my opinion, for a business to become someone's cause, it must transcend driving for success, or using the experience as a stepping-stone or making the endeavor only about financial success. I believe it's much more than that. It became a personal cause for me once we had flattened the clay on Parker's initial business model and created a vision for a new sculpture. We were willing to dream big, we were able to visualize something grander, and we did not want to compromise the scope of the sculpture by playing it safe when it came to what we truly wanted to create. Regardless of all the challenges, each accomplishment only fueled my investment in the vision and deepened my cause to help craft a masterwork.

It took numerous people to create the great success that WEX has enjoyed, and I am grateful to all of them and their efforts. However, as the book highlights, the trials and tribulations that WEX encountered were numerous, exciting, and character building. My longevity and roles with the company provided an unusual opportunity to influence the various phases, while navigating the many challenges we faced. I would like to believe that when I reached the position of CEO, I set a positive, steady, fair, and winning attitude that became embedded in the conscience of the company.

My wife once introduced me to a large audience and said, "With Mike, what you see is what you get." I think she is right. I've never purported to be something or someone that I am not. My values run deep and I'd like to believe they are rarely compromised. Furthermore, my personal and business life interactions and actions do not differ in any way. I like to believe in both cases that my value and respect for every human being is consistently demonstrated. I couldn't and wouldn't want it any other way.

As for the people of Maine, in my opinion they have depth of character, which includes persistence, compassion, integrity, and loyalty. They will work persistently to complete a task or tackle a challenge. They also demonstrate true care for the people they work with and for (i.e., customers) and they can be relied upon and trusted to not let you down. The people of Maine will be loyal to a cause if they are treated fairly and with respect. This made Maine a great fit for me and my character makeup. I have little tolerance for phoniness, but the people of Maine are authentic and we were able to build a real company, then drive its success, and create a culture where all of us who thrived in such an environment could commit ourselves and trust in the management and the culture we all built.

I reveled in this environment where I was able to develop and grow my career and hoped others at WEX felt some of the same feelings. So, when considering the saying that "the character of a business determines its fate," I think we had some built-in advantages in building a relationship-based B2B business in an environment where the ingredients for success were ever-present. All we had to do was unlock it by demonstrating a consistent level of trust and integrity, which was embraced and helped ignite the passions of the WEXers. Like all businesses with bold visions, our Road to WEXcellence was difficult, but thanks to great, passionate, and committed people the challenges were overcome. I thank and honor the great WEXers for the wonderful ride.

(Top): One of the original A.R. Wright family
business offices, Portland, Maine waterfront.
(Middle): Current WEX Headquarters,
South Portland, Maine
(Bottom Left): Logo prior to name change.
(Bottom Right): Current WEX Inc. logo

www.ingramcontent.com/pod-product-compliance
Lightning Source LLC
Chambersburg PA
CBHW060249220326
41598CB00027B/4033